BOOKMARKS ★

SOLIDARNOŠČ: THE MISSING LINK?

A NEW EDITION OF POLAND'S CLASSIC REVOLUTIONARY SOCIALIST MANIFESTO ★ KURON & MODZELEWSKI'S OPEN LETTER TO THE PARTY ★

★INTRODUCTION BY COLIN BARKER

This edition published May 1982 by Bookmarks,
265 Seven Sisters Road, Finsbury Park, London
N4 2DE.
'An Open Letter to the Party' was first published
in Poland in 1965. It was published in Britain in
1967 under the title 'A Revolutionary Socialist
Manifesto' by the International Socialists,
forerunners of the Socialist Workers Party.

ISBN O 906224 07 1

Printed by A Wheaton and Company, Exeter.
Design by Roger Huddle
Production by Artworkers

Published at the same time:
**SOLIDARNOSC: FROM GDANSK TO
MILITARY REPRESSION**
by Colin Barker and Kara Weber

★
CONTENTS

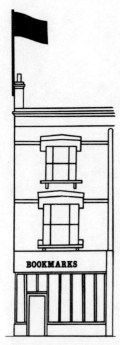

This is the sixth book to be published by the **Bookmarks Publishing Co-operative,** a group of socialists who have loaned money and contributed their skills.

Many socialists have a few savings put aside, probably in a bank or savings bank. While it's there, it's being loaned by the bank to some business or other to further the aims of capitalism. We believe that it is better loaned to a socialist venture to further the aims of socialism. In return for a loan to the **Bookmarks Publishing Co-operative,** repayable at a month's notice, members receive free copies of all books published, and other advantages which there isn't room here to mention.

Like to know more? Write to **Bookmarks Publishing Co-operative,** 265 Seven Sisters Road, London N4 2DE.

★ INTRODUCTION

IT IS an honour to be asked to introduce a new edition of Jacek Kuron and Karol Modzelewski's *Open Letter to the Party*. It is also a saddening experience. For the authors of this document have disowned their own ideas, with tragic consequences both for themselves and for the Polish working class.

In 1965, the day after they submitted their *Open Letter* to the Warsaw University Branch of the Polish United Workers Party, the two authors were arrested. Kuron was jailed for three years, Modzelewski for three and a half. They were charged with calling for the 'forcible overthrow of the political and socio-economic system of the People's Republic of Poland'. They were tried in chains. When the judgement was announced, they joined spectators in the court in singing the International. A copy of their document was smuggled to the West and published, and from this several socialist organisations published translations.[1]

Hardly had the authors been released from prison than the Polish student movement erupted in protest against the regime: they participated, and in 1968 were again arrested and imprisoned.

In the 1970s, Kuron in particular was centrally involved in a new opposition to the Polish regime, the Committee for Defence of Workers, KOR. KOR published a barrage of information about conditions in 'communist' Poland, and established contacts with militant workers in a number of industrial centres. Many of these workers were to play a leading role in the free trade union, Solidarity, which exploded onto the Polish scene in August 1980. Kuron and Modzelewski became advisers to the new workers' movement.

In December 1981, the Polish army under General Jaruzelski carried out a military coup which smashed Solidarity. Thousands of its working class leaders and its intellectual advisers and sympathisers were arrested and interned. Among them, again, were Kuron and Modzelewski. At the time of writing, the two authors and thousands of their comrades are still locked up in internment camps, and the whole Polish working class groans beneath the weight of a fierce military repression.

What is especially tragic about this situation is that the ideas that Kuron and Modzelewski had proposed in 1965 were immensely relevant to the workers' movement of 1980-81. As we have argued at length in *Solidarnosc: From Gdansk to Military Repression*[2], Solidarity was defeated unnecessarily: what brought it down was its adherence, almost to the very end, to a muddled reformist perspective and its lack of a clear set of revolutionary ideas. Kuron and Modzelewski themselves, and those around them, offered a form of political leadership within Solidarity that left it disarmed in the face of the regime. The tragedy of these courageous Marxist dissidents is that they had forgotten or abandoned the much better ideas that they had themselves once developed—those put forward in the pages which follow.

The significance of the *Open Letter to the Party* is threefold. First, the authors provided the basic outlines of a rigorous Marxist analysis of Poland and other East European societies, an analysis which they backed up with a wealth of empirical information. Second, they offered a clear and relevant argument for the necessity of revolutionary politics founded in the activity of the working class. Thirdly, they located their arguments in terms of a consistent socialist internationalism.

Each of these points deserves amplification.

For years, the working class movement across the whole world has been bedevilled by a terrible error: the belief that there is something 'socialist' about Russia and its East European satellites. Two generations of working class militants have seen it as their duty to defend the 'socialist' countries. This has placed them in the position of defending all manner of anti-working class actions and regimes.

Even among the left-oppositional currents—notably the uncritical followers of Leon Trotsky—who broke with the politics of subordination to the Kremlin, there persisted the idea that there was something more 'progressive' about the Russian and East European regimes. For these socialists the existence of 'state property' remained the crucial criterion. They suggested that, because Russia and its satellites had 'planned' economies in which the predominant property owner was the state, these countries remained socially superior to Western capitalism. For them, the question *which class controls* and *to what purposes?* became a subordinate issue. In the name of a misunderstood letter of Marxism, they killed its spirit; their judgements were no longer founded in the Marxist principle of working class self-emancipation.

Kuron and Modzelewski cut through these illusions. The character of Poland and the other 'communist' regimes, they insisted, is that of class society. Polish society is divided into two fundamentally opposed classes; one controls the means of production and exploits the other. The main exploited class is the working class, through whose exploitation the peasantry is also robbed. They called the exploiting class the 'central political bureaucracy'.

The idea that the 'communist' countries are class societies has found increasing favour with other critical socialist writers from both East and West. But most of these other critics have been content to remain at the level of description, without inquiring further into the mode of production that predominates in these countries. Kuron and Modzelewski's *Open Letter* stood out, in the dissident literature, by its theoretical rigour. The root of the problem, they suggested, is that the ruling class in Poland pursues a specific 'class goal' which it imposes on the rest of Polish society. That goal is 'production for the sake of production'; and it is to the endless pursuit of that goal that Polish society, its relations of production, its politics and its culture are forcibly subordinated.

Two points may be noted about this characterisation. First, Kuron and Modzelewski stressed that the goals of Poland's ruling class are different from, and opposed to, the interests of the mass of the Polish people and particular of the working classes. The fundamental need of the great majority is the development of production for the sake of consumption, production for the sake of human need. But, for the ruling class, the consumption needs of the working class are not the end in view; rather, they treat those consumption needs as merely a *cost* of production—and a cost they seek to keep as low as possible.

Second, the 'class goal' of the central political bureaucracy takes a definite social form. The ruling class's aim is not simply a high standard of consumption for themselves. Although, as a matter of fact, they live much better that the majority of the Polish people, this is a secondary matter. What is crucial is that they pursue 'production for the sake of production'. Kuron and Modzelewski, as Marxists, did not choose this phrase lightly. They took the term from Marx, who used it to define the key purpose of capitalist production.

'Except as capital personified, the capitalist has no historical value ... But, in so far as he is capital personified, his motivating force is not the acquisition and enjoyment of use-values, but the acquisition and augmentation of exchange-values. He is fanatically intent on the valorisation of value; consequently he ruthlessly forces the human race to produce for production's sake ...

'Accumulate, accumulate! That is Moses and the prophets! Therefore, save, save, re-convert the greatest possible portion of surplus-value or surplus-product into capital! Accumulation for the sake of accumulation, production for the sake of production ...'[3]

The bureaucracy, Kuron and Modzelewski emphasised, 'wants to increase capital, to enlarge the production apparatus, to accumulate' (page 26). Its class goal is the expansion of 'the surplus product in its physical form and the expansion of production, ie production for production's sake.'

It is, the authors insisted, this relentless pursuit of the expansion of national capital which produces the various tendencies to crisis in the Polish economy. Just as capital is prone to crisis in the West, so too in the East. The so-called 'planned economies' actually manifest various forms of crisis, including falling growth rates, inflation, balance of payments difficulties, waste production and the like, all of which Kuron and Modzelewski trace back to their roots in the mode of production.

The logic of the whole analysis which Kuron and Modzelewski offered, therefore, places their work in a particular tradition of criticism of the East European regimes, the tradition of 'state capitalist' analysis, developed in the West by such writers as Tony Cliff and Chris Harman.[4]

Kuron and Modzelewski's work was not only important for the general clarity of its exposition of the class character of Polish society. Their political conclusions were also of immense significance. Poland, they argued, is a society in crisis; and 'the economic crisis cannot be overcome within the framework of the present production relations ... A solution is possible only through the overthrow of prevailing production and social relations. *Production is a necessity for development.'* (page 66).

The crisis in Polish society, they suggested, pits every section of society in opposition to the ruling class. But the key social force in the necessary social revolution is the working class. Any realistic politics for the solution of the crisis of Polish society must rest on proletarian revolution. And they set out a programme of revolutionary demands through which a workers' revolution might be effected, centred on the need for workers' councils, workers' democracy and a workers' militia.

The problem posed by such a perspective is obvious: what will the Russians do, faced with a workers' revolution in Poland? To this the authors gave the only possible reply: the Polish revolution must seek its support in the struggles of the working classes of other countries, including the Russian workers. They offered no utopian and reactionary promises of 'socialism in one country': the workers' revolution must spread, not only elsewhere in Eastern Europe, but to the countries of Western capitalism too. 'Against an eventual accord between the international bureaucracy and the international imperialist bourgeoisie, which maintain systems of anti-popular dictatorship in their spheres of influence, we utter the traditional working class slogan: "proletarians of all countries, unite!" ' (page 81). Their whole work was thus marked by a consistent socialist internationalism, and an attack on all varieties of narrow reformism and nationalism.

The history of Poland since the writing of the *Open Letter to The Party* fully bore out the authors' prognoses. The crisis-tendencies they had analysed deepened. After 1970, in an effort to overcome the growing stagnation of the economy, the Gierek regime turned to the capitalist West for investment funds and markets, with a dual and contradictory result: production expanded very fast in the first half of the 1970s, and then ran sharply up against all the 'barriers' Kuron and Modzelewski had identified. Once more the crisis re-asserted itself, only this time on a massively expanded scale. By 1979, national output was actually falling; the years 1980 and 1981 saw the economy go into a major slump.[5]

In 1970, in 1976, and in 1980-81, the Polish working class rose in revolt against the regime. Especially, in 1980-81, the workers' organisation, Solidarity, demonstrated the capacity which Kuron and Modzelewski had predicted: it drew every section of exploited Polish society behind its magnificent banner. If ever there was an occasion in history when theory and practice had the opportunity to be linked indissolubly, the movement of 1980-81 offered it to the authors of the *Open Letter to the Party*.

The tragedy is that the authors of this superb revolutionary document did not develop their own arguments of the 1960s in practice. Instead, in 1980-81, they fell into the very trap they had themselves sharply criticised in 1965. In the *Open Letter*, they had looked back at the events of 1956, when a working class upsurge opened the way for all manner of revolutionary possibilities. That opportunity had been missed, they argued, because the 'October Left' of 1956 had misled the working class into coming to an accommodation with the liberal wing of the ruling bureaucracy. Instead of putting forward a revolutionary working class programme, the left had permitted the bureaucracy to escape from the political crisis, and to re-establish its grip on Polish society.

But, in the late 1970s and in the period of Solidarity's amazing rise after August 1980, Kuron and Modzelewski were no longer arguing for socialist revolution in Poland. No longer were they warning against 'political realism', criticising the role of the Church, warning against the regular Army. How tragically prophetic their words of 1956 now sound! 'The regular army, like the political police, is by its very nature of a tool of antidemocratic dictatorship. As long as it is maintained, a clique of Generals may always prove stronger than all the parties and councils' (page 77).

Instead of urging the formation of a revolutionary party to show the working class the way forward, they were urging the workers not go to "too far'. What was needed, they said, echoing the reformist phrase of the Western 'Eurocommunists', was a 'historic compromise' between the workers and their class enemy, the central political bureaucracy.

For Kuron and Modzelewski and their co-thinkers in 1980 and 1981, the militancy and insurgency of Solidarity's millions of working class members had become 'a problem'. They no longer sought to provide militant leadership to the workers' movement, but to encourage a 'self-limiting revolution', avoiding at all costs an open confrontation with the state and the ruling class. Thus their politics became those of working class de-mobilisation.

Alas, the same reformist politics have been tried before, too many times. Kuron and Modzelewski's *Open Letter* itself referred to the betrayal of the 1936 revolution in Spain and to the debacles in France, Italy and Greece after the Second World War. More recently, the same reformist politics were attempted in Chile—with the military coup of 1973 as the bloody outcome. In December 1981, in Poland, the military again gave brutal evidence of the limits of 'self-limiting revolution'. The army smashed Solidarity, forced down working class living standards, and violently re-imposed the bureaucracy's class goals on the Polish workers. Once again, the path of 'compromise' had led to disaster. As in 1956 in Poland, so in 1980-81: the Left pursued policies which brought defeat to the working class.

The saddest aspect of all this is that it need not have been so. Jacek Kuron and Karol Modzelewski had won the personal right, by their courage and their activity, to offer leadership to the Polish working class. But they had 'forgotten' their own best arguments. Socialists must now offer them unconditional solidarity against Jaruzelski's butchers and jailers. But, because we must look also to the future, the most serious fraternal criticism is also demanded.

The *Open Letter to the Party,* this brilliant work of 1965, has now passed into the collective possession of the socialist movement. We re-publish it now as a small contribution to fulfilling the hope that, when next the Polish workers rise, some among them will remember the strengths of the revolutionary argument.

Colin Barker
February 1982

NOTES

1 An earlier edition of this text was published in Britain in 1967 by the International Socialists, forerunners of the Socialist Workers Party.

2 Colin Barker and Kara Weber, *Solidarnosc: From Gdansk to Military Repression* (International Socialism 15) Spring 1982.

3 Karl Marx, *Capital,* Vol I (Harmondsworth: Penguin Books), pp 739-42

4 There is a theoretical ambiguity in the *Open Letter* which has enabled the work to be claimed also for the different, and theoretically weaker, theory of 'bureaucratic collectivism' (for example, by Antonio Carlo, 'The Socio-Economic Nature of the USSR' *Telos* 21). Kuron and Modzelewski employ the terminology appropriate to capitalist production, but they don't sufficiently identify the social mechanism by which the 'class goal' of accumulation and production for production's sake is imposed upon the bureaucracy. In capitalism, Marx wrote, 'competition subordinates every individual capitalist to the immanent laws of capitalist production, as external and coercive laws. It compels him to keep extending his capital, so as to preserve it, and he can only extend it by means of progressive accumulation' (*Capital*, I, p 739). In Poland, as Kuron and Modzelewski say, all enterprises are owned by the one state, and there are no competitive relations between them. So, if the categories of Marx's *Capital* are applicable to Poland, there must be some mechanism whereby, through competition, the bureaucracy's 'class goal' is forced on them. The authors provide only a hint of such a mechanism:

> 'The material power of the bureaucracy, the scope of its authority over production, its international position (very important for a class organised as a group identifying itself with the state) all this depends on the size of the national capital. Consequently, the bureaucracy wants to increase capital, to enlarge the producing apparatus, to accumulate' (page 26).

> There is a germ of an idea here which needs development: that it is international rivalry which provides the missing mechanism through which Polish production is subordinated to accumulation. That is, the class relations within Poland's frontiers, the form of exploitation and class struggle, can only be understood if we see Poland in its *world* context. The argument is further developed in Tony Cliff *State Capitalism in Russia* (London: Pluto Press), 1974. See also Chris Harman, *Bureaucracy and Revolution in Eastern Europe,* (London: Pluto Press) 1974.

5 See Barker and Weber, *op cit,* Part II, for an extended discussion.

1.
THE RULE OF THE BUREAUCRACY

ACCORDING TO OFFICIAL doctrine, we live in a socialist country. This thesis is based on the identification of state ownership of the means of production with social ownership. The act of nationalization transferred industry, transport, and banking into social property, and production relations based on social property are allegedly socialist.

This reasoning is Marxist in appearance. In reality, an element fundamentally alien to Marxist theory has been introduced: the formal, legal meaning of ownership. State ownership can conceal various class meanings, depending on the class character of the state. The public sector in the economies of contemporary capitalist countries has nothing in common with social ownership. This is true not only because there exist, beside it, private capitalist corporations, but because the worker in a capitalist state factory is totally deprived of ownership, since he has no real influence in the state and hence no control over his own labor and its product. History has seen examples of class and antagonistic societies in which state ownership of the means of production has prevailed (the so-called Asiatic method of production).

State ownership of the means of production is only a *form* of ownership. It is exercised by those social groups to which the state belongs. In a nationalized economic system, only those who participate in, or can influence decisions of an economic nature (such as use of the means of production, the distribution of, and profiting from the product) can affect the decisions of the state. Political power is connected with power over the process of production and the distribution of the product.

To whom does power belong in our state? To one monopolistic Party—the Polish United Workers' Party (PUWP). All essential decisions are made first in the Party, and only later in the offices of the official state power; no important decision can be made and carried out without the approval of the Party authorities. This is called the leading role of the Party, and since the monopolistic Party considers itself the representative of the interests of the working class, its power is supposed to be a guarantee of working class power.

But if we are not to evaluate the system according to what its leaders think and say about themselves, then we must see what opportunities there are for the working class to influence the decisions of the state apparatus.

Outside the Party—none. For the ruling Party is monopolistic. It is impossible for the working class to organize in other parties and, through them, to formulate, propagate and struggle for the realization of other programs, other variants of dividing the national product, political concepts other than those of the PUWP. The prohibition by the ruling Party against organizing the working class is guarded by the entire state apparatus of power and force: the administration, political police, attorney general's office, the courts, and also the political organizations led by the Party, which unmask and nip in the bud all attempts to undermine the leading role of the PUWP.

But more than a million Party members are ordinary citizens; among them, several hundred thousand are workers. What are their chances of influencing the decisions of Party and state authorities? The Party is not only monopolistic, but is also organized along monolithic lines. All factions, groups with different platforms, organized political currents, are forbidden within the Party. Every rank-and-file member is entitled to his opinion, but he has no right to organize others who think as he does to follow his program, and he has no right to organize a propaganda and electoral struggle for the realization of that program. Elections to Party offices, to conferences and congresses become fictitious under such conditions, since they do not take place on the basis of different programs and platforms (i.e., an assessment of political alternatives). Exercising political initiative in society demands organization, but in any attempt to exert influence on the decisions of the "top," the mass of rank-and-file Party members is deprived of organization, atomized, therefore powerless. The only source of political initiative can be—in the nature of things—organized bodies, i.e., the (Party) apparatus. Like every apparatus, it is organized hierarchically; information flows upward, while decisions and orders are handed down from above. As in every hierarchical apparatus, the fountainhead of orders is the élite, the group of people who occupy conspicuous positions in the hierarchy and who collectively make basic decisions.

In our system, the Party élite is, at one and the same time, also the power élite; all decisions relating to state power are made by it and, in any case, at the top of the Party and state hierarchies there exists, as a rule, a fusion of responsible posts. By exercising state power, the Party élite has at its disposal all the nationalized means of production; it decides on the extent of accumulation and consumption, on the direction of investment, on the share of various social groups in consumption and in the national income; in other words, it decides on the distribution and utilization of the entire social product. The decisions of the élite are independent, free of any control on the part of the working class and of the remaining classes and social strata. The workers have no way of influencing them, nor have Party members in general. Elections to the Sejm and National Councils become fictitious, with only one list of candidates drawn up by the "top" and a lack of any real differences in the programs of the PUWP and the satellite parties (United Peasant Party and Democratic Party). This Party-state power élite, free of any social control and able independently to make all key economic decisions of nation-wide importance (as well as all political decisions), we shall call the *central political bureaucracy*.

Membership in the central political bureaucracy is determined by real participation in reaching basic political and economic decisions that are made centrally and are effective on a national scale. It is probably impossible to draw the exact limits of this élite. Fixing its exact limits would require sociological research in an area which is completely taboo. For us, however, the most important thing is not the numerical strength and internal organization of the bureaucracy, but its role in society and in the social process of production.

If the rank-and-file of the Party is disorganized in terms of influencing the decisions of the bureaucracy it is organized to execute the bureaucracy's orders according to the principles of Party discipline. Whoever opposes it is removed, and outside the Party he has no right to organize and therefore to act. In this way the Party, which at the top of its hierarchy is simply the organized bureaucracy, becomes at the "bottom" a tool for disrupting attempts at resistance by the working class, while at the same time organizing the working class and other social groups in a spirit of obedience to the bureaucracy. The same function is fulfilled by the remaining social organizations directed by the Party, including the trade unions. The traditional organization of workers' economic self-defense, subjected to the leadership of the only organized political force, i.e., the Party, has become an obedient organ of the bureaucracy, that is of state power, both political and economic.

The bureaucracy thus exercises the totality of political and economic power, depriving the working class not only of the means of power and control, but even of self-defense. The leaders of the bureaucracy, at the same time, consider themselves spokesmen for the interests of the working class. If we are not to evaluate the system according to the statements of its leaders, we must analyze the class nature of the bureaucracy. The fact that it exercises power is not conclusive. It is the relationships of production that are decisive; we must, therefore, examine more carefully the productive process and the relationships in that process between the working class, which is the basic creator of the national income, and the central political bureaucracy, which collectively has at its disposal the means of production.

2.
WAGES, SURPLUS PRODUCT, PROPERTY

WHO CREATES THE NATIONAL INCOME and how is it being shared? According to Marxist theory, the national income originates in the area of material production, that is, in industry, construction, partly in transport, agriculture, and the craft trades. In industry, the creator of the national income is the so-called collective worker, that is, the sum total of workers who prepare, execute and guarantee the technical productive process. Hence, apart from workers employed directly or indirectly in the productive process, this also includes the technicians, designers, and the technical intelligentsia. On the other hand, men who are not engaged in the process of production, but whose job consists of supervising relationships between people engaged in that process, i.e., supervisors of wage labor, the technocrats, are not considered productive workers. It is true that they, too, insure production in the same sense in which this was done in the past by the ancient slave driver or the feudal overseer of serfs or a contemporary capitalist factory manager. Their job, however, is to insure the existing production relations and not the material productive process itself.

In agriculture, the productive workers, i.e., the creators of national income, are the individual peasants, the State Farm workers, and the peasants associated in Producers' Cooperatives, rather few in Poland, while in the municipal small manufacturing sector, they are the craftsmen.

Lately the thesis has been advanced that the Marxist concept which limits the creation of the national income to the area of material production is out of date and that today all those who work create the national income. For in the sector of services (i.e., outside the area of material production), the needs of production and consumption are indirectly met. The life of the community is organized, in other words, through a given amount of work. In this way the essential needs of society are met.

Such reasoning would be legitimate only in a society in which an equivalent exchange of production and services takes place—in other words, on condition that the producer of material goods gets in return, in the form of services provided him exclusively, the equivalent of that part of the product of his labor which he provides for the support of the services sector, while at the same time accumulation is subordinated to his interests. If these conditions are not fulfilled, then to treat all work (hence also the work of the policeman, the prosecutor, the officer and the hotelkeeper) as productive labor effectively covers up exploitation. The entire national income, except the part destined for accumulation, could then be reduced to the wages of different types of workers, i.e., the remuneration for "productive" work. In the same way, one could cover up exploitation in contemporary capitalist societies. Apart from individual consumption of material goods by the capitalist class (which amounts to a small fraction of the social product and only a small part of the income of that class) all that is left of the national income would be reduced to the wages and incomes of the producers of material goods, to the wages of other workers employed directly by the capitalists or by the state, and to the accumulation fund. Such reasoning would have nothing in common with an objective, scientific analysis and everything in common with apologetics.

We accept such categories of reasoning which can serve to analyze real contradictions, not conceal them. That is why we assume, following Marx's example, that the national income is the objectivized labor of productive workers in the sector of material goods production; the basis of accumulation and "services," broadly taken, is the material product created in this sector. Hence the creation of the accumulation fund and expenses for the police, armed forces, culture, health services, etc.—this amounts to making use of the national income created outside those services, which the worker has paid for out of his own pocket, while all the rest is supported from the unpaid part of the worker's or peasant's labor, i.e., from the surplus product. We must, therefore, look more closely at the distribution of that product in order to be able to say in whose interest its various parts are utilized.

The fundamental groups of creators of the national income in our country are the workers and the individual peasants. How do they participate in sharing the product of their labor?

Individual peasants place the products of their labor on the market. But 75% of the production of peasant farms is marketed through state agencies, which buy these products at prices which are, on the average, 40% below market prices. Moreover the state, being in fact a monopolist in the market place, determines prices for agricultural produce in a way which is unfavorable to the peasant in relation to industrial products. We shall drop this matter for the moment, but shall return to it in our analysis of the situation in agriculture.

The workers participate in sharing the national product in an amount which is determined, above all, by their *working wage*. What is the working wage in our country and what does its size depend on?

ACCORDING TO PROFESSOR KALECKI'S ESTIMATE, the worker's real income for the same type work he did before the war averaged 45% higher in 1960 than in 1937. That increase is higher than the increase in real wages for the same work because of the higher rate of collective consumption and secondary employment in addition to the worker's regular job. The postwar statistics understate the cost of living by ignoring the hidden rise in prices. But we shall accept Professor Kalecki's estimate as roughly correct. The wage increase during the period of 1949–1960 took place for the most part in 1956–1959. It was not a normal period for the system but one of political crisis, upheaval in the Party's monolithic structure, strikes and broad collective demands for wage increases and, for a short period, of flourishing Workers' Councils elected by the work crews and independent (until 1958) of the Party apparatus. Because of all these factors, the power apparatus was relatively weak and society comparatively strong. Under those circumstances, the working class, in less than four years, gained a 30% increase in real wages and at least three-fourths of its increase over 1937. It is difficult to find any real increase in wages during the period 1949–1956; the same applies to the period after 1959. According to the Central Statistical Office (CSO) analysis of family budgets for the past four years (1960–1963), the worker's real family income increased by 2.5%. But taking into consideration the hidden price rise, not included in the official statistics, we conclude that over the past four years the average worker's family standard of living not only failed to rise, but fell somewhat.

On the other hand, the value of the gross industrial product, at world market prices, was nearly 9 times that of the 1938 (and 1948) product, and national income grew from 1949 to 1963 by over 2.5 times. Owing to increased employment, the increase in per capita consumption was higher in the period 1949–1960 than the modest increase in real wages would suggest. But that is observed in every system as the result of growing industrialization. The so-called rate of exploitation does not depend upon the volume of employment but upon the ratio of the value of the manufactured product to the wages of the workers who produced it. The national income produced by the worker has been growing disproportionately faster than the modest increase in his wages (the latter having been won mostly during the few years when conditions were abnormal for the system). During the years 1960–1962, industrial production grew by 20% (net) while the worker's wages grew less than 5%; at the same time, according to official statistics, food prices grew by 3.4% in the nationalized stores, by 7% in restaurants, and by 12% on the free market. As we have seen, the standard of living for working class families did not show any increase at all.

Polish food physiologists established 4 norms for meat consumption. Norm A, hardly adequate and not recommended for a long period, requires a monthly per capita average of 3.7 Kg. Norm B, adequate and permitting a normal functioning of the organism over a long period, requires 4 Kg. The data on family budgets reveals that in about 23% of working class families the consumption of meat and meat products is below the hardly adequate norm, and in 18 to 19% of such families, it is within the hardly adequate norm but still below the adequate norm.

According to a research project conducted at the Warsaw Motorcycle Factory in 1957, 23% of the workers ate meat for dinner once a week or less, and 25% ate it twice a week. One might suppose that data seven years old are no longer true, but in fact consumption of meat and meat products in 1957 was 43.9 kilograms, a level higher than that of 1960 (42.5 kilograms) and not much below that of 1962 (45.8 kilograms).

The subsistence minimum includes not only food consumption but clothing, shelter, elementary comforts and household furnishings as well. In 1957, the corresponding average figures per worker investigated at the Warsaw Motorcycle Factory were as follows: 51% of a woolen suit; 105% of a suit of low percentage fibers; 80% of a separate pair of pants; 60%

of a separate jacket. In the lowest income group (18% of the total number investigated), there was one woolen suit for every five workers. As for winter clothing, the average worker had 15% of a woolen winter overcoat, 12% of a winter overcoat of low percentage fibers, 20% of a woolen topcoat and 50% of a topcoat of low percentage fibers. One might suppose that since then the situation has improved markedly. But according to official data, average real wages increased from 1958 to 1963 by about 12%, and it is a certainty that workers' real wages increased by less than the general average figure. (From 1960 to 1963, the average real income of people employed in industry grew by 4.5%, workers' families by 2.5%.)

Ten per cent of the investigated families at the Warsaw Motorcycle Factory had less than 3 square meters of living space per person; the next 19% had 3 to 4 sq. meters per person; the next 10% had 4 to 5 sq. meters, and another 13% had 5 to 6 sq. meters per person. (Altogether 52% of the families had less than 6 sq. meters of living space.) Only 1% of the apartments had hot running water, and 46% had cold running water, 25% had a water closet in the apartment, 7% had a bathroom in the building. There was 30% of a bed per person for the average family under investigation; 65% of the workers suffered chronic diseases.

According to the CSO data on workers' family budgets, up to the third income group (600 to 800 zloty per month) all income increase goes first of all into increased consumption of meat and meat products, milk and milk products, eggs, sugar and similar food commodities. Only from the third income group up do expenditures on those commodities grow more slowly than the family income and expenses on clothing, education, cultural needs and sports, faster. This means that in the third income group, satisfaction of most elementary needs reaches what workers' families consider to be the subsistence minimum. About 22–23% of workers' families live below that level. This corresponds approximately to those whose meat consumption is below the minimum norm.

The subsistence minimum involves people living in society, hence it is subject to change. It is socially and historically conditioned and grows with the growth of industry, technology and the general cultural level in any given society. Development of modern industry requires workers with additional qualifications on a higher cultural level and, consequently, have greater cultural needs, spiritual as well as material. The workers' subsistence minimum today is no doubt higher than it was in 1937. Similar progress takes place in capitalist countries and in most West European countries the workers' real income increased during the past 25–30 years no less than 45%. Nevertheless, the workers' wages did not cease to represent what they did a quarter century ago: the equivalent of an historically-shaped subsistence minimum or, in other words, the price of labor power.

As IS EVIDENT FROM THIS ANALYSIS of family budgets provided by the Central Statistical Office, differences in consumption levels among workers' families result, not so much from differences in wage levels but, above all, from differences in the size of each family and the number of wage earners per family. It shows that, at present, the average wage in our country prevents one-quarter of workers' families from attaining a minimum standard of living, due to the size of those families, while a further 13% of workers' families can only maintain themselves with this average wage at a level not exceeding the accepted minimum standard of living. Above the minimum, we find mainly childless married couples and families with one or, at most, two children (provided that both parents are wage earners). This means that the worker's wage in our country corresponds to the *historically determined minimum of existence.* In other words, the worker's wage allows him to take part in the sharing of the national income only insofar as it is necessary for him to survive and bring up his offspring, i.e., to reproduce his own labor power and prepare new workers for industry.

The worker's wage is, therefore, only a *part of production costs,* one that is just as indispensable as investments for raw materials and machines.

As a rule, the worker has the advantage of living very inexpensively in a government-owned building. His lodging is therefore part free. But to live and produce he must stay somewhere. At any rate, his apartment rarely has any luxuries and in most cases not even the elementary comforts. It is part of his subsistence minimum, supplied to him in addition to his wages.

The workers receive medical care free and can buy medicines at a discount, but these are necessary in order to preserve his labor power: they are ingredients of his subsistence minimum. If free medical care were abolished and rents increased, the worker's wages would have to be raised in proportion to the increase in his necessary expenses. These non-returnable benefits and services are a necessary part of the worker's subsistence minimum, a wage supplement as necessary to the worker as the wages themselves, and therefore a constituent of production cost.

In proportion to the worker's wages, those services and benefits are of secondary importance. Their per capita annual value of collective consumption amounts to only 1,200 zloty.

What part of the product created by the worker makes up his working wage? Official statistics give a distorted picture for two reasons: 1) prices, on the basis of which production in Department A (production of the means of production) is calculated, are not real prices but aggregates, and they are calculated at a very low rate in relation to production in Department B (production of consumer goods), which falsely increase the share of the worker's labor in the end product. 2) The artificial lowering of prices for agricultural produce underplays agriculture's role and exaggerates the part played by industry in creating national income.

Out of necessity, however, we have used, in our paper, official statistics, treating the results thus obtained only as an approximate illustration of reality.

In 1962, the productive worker in industry created, on the average, a product worth 71,000 zloty, out of which he received, as a working wage, a monthly average of 2,200 zloty. In other words, for one-third of the working day, the worker creates a subsistence minimum for himself. and for the remaining two-thirds, the surplus product.

The working class has no influence on the size of the surplus product, on its use and distribution, since—as we have seen—it is deprived of influence on the decisions of the authorities, who have at their disposal the means of production and the labor product itself. It is not the working class that fixes the working wage—that wage is imposed from above, just as are the production norms (at one and the same time). The workers have no rights of, and no way of engaging in, economic self-defense, since, as already noted, they are deprived of any organization of their own, and any effective strike action must be organized. Any organization of workers aimed at carrying on a struggle for higher wages is illegal and, as such, prosecuted by the power apparatus—the police, attorney general's office, and the courts. The surplus product is thus taken away by force from the working class in proportions that have not been fixed by the workers, and is then made use of outside the range of their influence and possibility of control.

What purpose does the surplus product serve? First, it is used for capital accumulation, i.e., for expanding production. But since the worker receives only the minimum for existence, the purpose of his production is not his class goal. Similarly, under capitalism, production may correspond to the worker's interest to the extent that it provides him with a job from which he earns a living; for all that, production is by no means his own goal. In the prevailing system, expenditure for accumulation serves a purpose which is alien to the worker. Second, it is used to support the apparatus of coercion (army, political police, prisons etc.) which perpetuates the present economic and social relationships.

Third, expenditures are financed from the surplus product in sectors whose function, to all appearances, is not connected with the class nature of the system (science, education, universities, culture, health, various services). These sectors undoubtedly fulfill a general social purpose, but that purpose is fulfilled by culture, education, and science, and also by the very production of material goods, in any antagonistic society, which does not thereby lose its class nature. In the expenditures discussed above, three general goals may be distinguished:

1) expenditures which directly serve production

2) expenditures which indirectly serve as an apologia for the prevailing social relationships and the process of implanting in the consciousness of the people the required norms of collective living

3) expenditures for various kinds of non-repayable services and benefits for the working class and the mass of hired laborers.

IF THE PRODUCT CREATED BY THE WORKER does not belong to him, it means that his labor—which creates that product—does not belong to him either. Why is this so?

In order to live, the worker must produce. In order for production to continue, there must be a fusion of labor power and the means of production. The worker disposes only of his own labor, but he does not have the means of production at his disposal. The fusion of his labor with the means of production belonging to others can, therefore, take place only through contact between the worker, as the owner of the labor power, and the owners of the means of production on the labor market. The worker is thus exploited, because he is deprived of the *ownership of the means of production*; in order to live, he must *sell his labor*. From the moment he performs that act, which to him is indispensable, i.e., when he sells his ability to do a given job in a given time, his labor and its product no longer belong to him but to those who have bought his labor, the owners of the means of production, the exploiters.

To whom does the worker in our country sell his labor? To those who have at their disposal the means of production, in other words, to the *central political bureaucracy*. On account of this, the central political bureaucracy is the ruling class; it has at its exclusive command the basic means of production; it buys the labor of the working class; it takes away from the working class by force and economic coercion the surplus product and uses it for purposes that are alien and hostile to the worker in order to strengthen and expand its rule over production and society.

It is said that the bureaucracy cannot be a class, since the individual earnings of its members do not come anywhere near the individual earnings of capitalists; since no bureaucrat, taken by himself, rules anything more than his mansion, his car, and his secretary; since entrance to the bureaucratic ranks is determined by a political career and not by inheritance; and since it is relatively easy to be eliminated from the bureaucracy in a political showdown. This is quite wrong. All the above arguments prove only the obvious: the property of the bureaucracy is not of an individual nature, but constitutes the collective property of an élite which identifies itself with the state. This fact defines the principle of the bureaucracy's internal organization, but its class character does not depend on its internal organization or its mores, only on its relationship—as a group—to the means of production and to other social classes (above all, the working class). The individual earnings of capitalists are incomparably greater than the earnings of bureaucrats. But capitalists, from their individual earnings, set aside an investment fund, pay the overseers of their hired labor and those employees who serve them personally or whose task it is to strengthen their prestige and authority; they gain status, influence, and political power thanks to their individual earnings. From its individual earnings the bureaucracy covers only part of its direct personal consumption, while all that remains— the investment fund, funds for supporting the countless numbers of people whose task it is to protect its rule, to make propaganda for the system, to supervise the workers, etc.—is taken from the revenue of the state, which remains at its exclusive disposal.

In view of the limited numerical strength of the bureaucratic class, its consumption of luxury articles takes up only a fractional part of the social product, but in the capitalist system, too, the personal consumption of the capitalists takes up only an insignificant part of that product. This is not the essence of exploitation, for direct personal consumption is not an end in itself of the ruling class under any system. The privilege of high consumption, prestige and power, as well as all other social privileges result from the ability to command production. Hence every ruling class aims at maintaining, strengthening and expanding its command over production and over society; to that end, it uses the surplus product, and to that purpose it subordinates the very process of production.

3.
THE CLASS PURPOSE OF PRODUCTION

EACH RULING CLASS SETS THE GOALS of social production. It does so in its own class interest, that is, in the interest of strengthening and extending its authority over production and society.

The position of an individual capitalist (of a corporation, a monopoly, etc.) in society depends on the size of its capital, just as the international position of the capitalist class of a given country depends on the amount of national capital. For capital is the contemporary form of ruling over labor and its product. The aim of the capitalist, therefore, is first of all to increase or accumulate his capital.

The capitalist acquires all elements necessary for production on the market: machines, raw materials, labor. He must, therefore, sell all his manufactured products on the market. For him, the goal of production is not the surplus product itself in its physical form but a maximum profit, the maximum difference between his total expenditure on production (machines, raw materials and labor) and the price obtained on the market for the whole product.

The contradiction between the tendency to accumulate capital and the low consumption of the working class arises in the very process of production. It manifests itself on the market as a disproportion between the growth of capital and the social product and the low purchasing power of the masses. In free-competition capitalism this contradiction was regulated by cyclical crises; in contemporary capitalism, by business fluctuations and, in certain cases, by a slower rate of growth, a decrease in productive capacity, production of armaments and by state expenditure which, to a certain degree, makes production independent of the market; finally, by an increase of consumption by the so-called middle class and by the working class organized into parties and unions, which fight for increased wages and social benefits. However, if the statistics show that for certain longer periods of time the share of capital and labor in the distribution of the national income is more or less stable, this does not mean that the goal of production has changed. Maximum profit remains the goal and the increase of consumption by the working class is a necessary evil, unavoidable for political or economic reasons.

In our system, individual capitalists do not exist. The factories, foundries, mines and their entire production belong to the state. Since the state finds itself in the hands of a central political bureaucracy—the collective owner of the means of production and the exploiter of the working class—all means of production and maintenance have become one centralized national "capital." The material power of the bureaucracy, the scope of its authority over production, its international position (very important for a class organized as a group identifying itself with the state) all this depends on the size of the national capital. Consequently, the bureaucracy wants to increase capital, to enlarge the producing apparatus, to accumulate.

What is the class goal of the bureaucracy, implemented in the very production process? What is the class purpose of production? It is not the profit of the given enterprise but the surplus product on a national scale. For it provides both the means for capital accumulation and the investments needed to maintain and strengthen the rule of the bureaucracy. As opposed to the capitalist, the bureaucracy does not need to achieve its surplus product in the market place, nor that part of the total product which corresponds to the depreciation of the fixed capital. It is the owner of all industrial plants and their production, and therefore does not need to buy anything from itself. If the transfer of steel from a foundry to a mill or of coal from a mine to a foundry is entered in the ledgers as the purchase of the means of production, then, in reality, it is simply a form of registering the transfer of a product within the bounds of the same property and not a real act of buying and selling. As proof, we have the fact that prices within the nationalized sector are of a purely agreed-upon nature. They are only a tool that serves to count goods, hence their relationships need not correspond to the relationships between the values of the goods.

The only element of production which the bureaucracy does not possess is labor power. The bureaucracy buys it "en bloc," under monopolistic conditions (behind every factory there is the same owner, so the worker always "chooses" the same buyer, who does not permit him to organize for the defense of his own economic interests), but even so, it buys it on the market. It is a real act of buying and selling and the worker must be paid. Only with what? With money of course, but we know that banknotes in this system have a different meaning for the bureaucracy than they have for the capitalist—they are simply a means of controlling the process of sharing the product, this being in the hands of the bureaucracy. The size of the working wage simply determines the level of living standards at the disposal of the bureaucracy which it passes on to the worker as the equivalent of his labor.

In fact, the bureaucracy pays for labor with a certain amount of means of subsistence by producing consumer goods, building apartments, hospitals, nurseries, etc., as well as by producing food. Where the land is owned individually the products of the soil are not the property of the bureaucracy and it must buy them on the market from the peasant producer. In this case also there is a monopolistic market in which the bureaucracy determines prices for peasants' products at a disadvantage for them in comparison with industrial prices. Nevertheless, it is a real act of sale and purchase and the peasant must be paid. With what? Again, with the production of consumer goods and of industrial tools for the cultivation of the soil. The food bought from the peasants represents part of the workers' minimum subsistence. Therefore, the price paid to the peasant is part of the expense of the purchase of labor for industry, construction, transport and the non-productive sectors. The price of labor is therefore derived from the production of consumer goods, the building of apartments, hospitals, etc., and the production of agricultural machinery.

As we have seen, labor power is the only element of the productive process that the bureaucracy does not own directly. The purchase of labor or the production of "Department B" (consumer goods) is, from the bureaucracy's point of view, the only necessary expense for keeping production operating and the surplus product coming in. Striving to obtain the maximum surplus product, the bureaucracy keeps this expense at the lowest possible level. Production for consumption is, from its class point of view, a necessary evil, whereas production for production is its goal.

When we look at production as a process between man and nature, as a natural process existing in every society, it cannot be an aim in itself. It is always production for consumption. For it is a conscious activity, caused by a need, and consumption of the material goods recreates the need.

The subjective and private goal of a ruling class (class goal of production) may be opposed to this general social goal of production. This occurs in capitalist society as well as in the bureaucratic, in view of the specific tendency of ruling classes to increase production and, simultaneously, to narrow distribution on class lines, thereby limiting consumption. In both systems this contradiction limits production itself, but in different ways.

To achieve his goals, maximum profit and its accumulation, a capitalist must sell the goods he produces on the market. The nature of the product makes no difference to him as long as the market absorbs it. In the last analysis, this production is directed at the consumer. Therefore, the effective demand, conditioned by the level of social consumption, determines the possibilities of market capacity and, by the same token, restrains capitalist production and accumulation through periodic crises or other difficulties in selling manufactured products.

In the section on the economic crisis of the system, we explained how a low level of social consumption limits production in a bureaucratic system. We would like to expand on that. It does not happen through the mechanism of the market. For the class goal of the bureaucracy is not profit and its accumulation, but the surplus product in its physical form and the expansion of production, i.e. production for production's sake. What enters the market is only labor power and the means of maintaining it, not the surplus product or the part of it which serves to recreate and enlarge constant capital (machinery, raw materials, fuel, etc.). The market does not regulate production. Therefore, cyclical crises of business or limitations of production through marketing difficulties cannot occur. As a result, it is possible to maintain for a long period an extremely high rate of accumulation and growth of industrial production while consumption remains low. The contradiction between the class goal of production and consumption becomes manifest in this system before the start of the production cycle, at the planning stage. Usually in economic planning one presupposes the highest possible level of accumulation, i.e., the lowest possible share of consumption of the national income because of the greater increase of production in Department A than in Department B. This disproportion becomes greater during the realization of the plans: as a rule the execution of the investment plan is threatened and there is a tendency to carry out the plan at the expense of consumption. Consequently, the area of accumulation increases and the area of consumption decreases. The increase of production in Department A is accordingly higher and in Department B lower.

IT IS EVIDENT THAT, despite this, an increase in the national income is usually accompanied by an increase in consumption. This results from the growth of employment and (in far lesser degree) from an improvement in the minimum level of existence. During certain periods, the proportion of consumption in the national income can be stable or can even grow (especially under the influence of a direct political threat by the working class). This does not mean, however, that the class goal of production has changed: the bureaucracy treats the growth of consumption as a necessary evil and the surplus product remains the goal. As with every economic law, production for the sake of production and inflated accumulation remain a trend and not an absolute rule.

Over longer periods, this tendency shows up in statistics. In 1949, which can rightly be taken as the starting point because it marks the end of the period of reconstruction and the consolidation of economic, social and political conditions into the system of bureaucratic dictatorship, the share of consumption in the national income was 85% and the share of accumulation—15%. In 1963, the share of consumption was 74.6% and accumulation—25.4%. This tendency was not realized in a uniform manner. In 1950, there was a rapid increase of accumulation from 15% to 20% and in 1953 it reached an all time high—27.1% of the national income. Then it grew more slowly (22.4% in 1954). In 1956-1957, the share of accumulation went down, respectively, to 19.7% and 21.5% and in 1960, another jump occurred, from 21.9% to 24.2%. After that, there is a tendency for it to increase: in 1961-1963 consumption increased by barely 15% (individual consumption by only 12%) and accumulation by 23%, according to official statistics. General consumption increased in addition to individual consumption—what official statistics call "remaining consumption," i.e., material expenditures for unproductive sectors of the economy—from the military and the police to nurseries and kindergartens.

The share of individual consumption in the national income in 1949 was 77.8% and in 1963—66.1%. (The lowest during the last 20 years, since even in 1953 it was 66.9%). We must also remember that the prices of the means of production in which accumulation is calculated have, among us, a putative character and are calculated on the basis of low consumer goods prices. If we accept the level of consumption in 1949 as 100, then the figures for 1963 were: 361 for accumulation and 215 for consumption. The smaller percentage of accumulation in 1956-1957 coincides with the political crisis, the weakening of the state power and the pressure on wages. Other than that, from 1949 on there is a hardly interrupted increase of accumulation in the national income along with decreased consumption. Due to large investments planned for 1966-1970, there will be a further tendency in the same direction. We can see then that the tendency toward "production for production" is not myth, but reality.

In our consideration of the class purpose of production, we have completely ignored the personal consumption of the bureaucrats. In view of the small size of the central political bureaucracy, its consumption takes up such a tiny part of the total product that the goals of production cannot be affected. But from the surplus product, the bureaucracy supports a great army of officials, propagandists, managers, policemen and so on, who serve to maintain and strengthen the production and social relationships on which its rule is based.

This throng consumes its part of the national income and contains privileged groups with a high level of consumption. The most important undoubtedly is the technocracy, in view of the connection between its functions and the productive process. Is it not the case then that the goal of production is also, partially, that of satisfying the needs of the apparatus, with the managers of industrial enterprises at its head? Does this mean that the bureaucracy is not the ruling class but merely serves the ambitions of privileged social groups, just as the power élite in the capitalist countries is, in fact, the political representative of the great monopolistic bourgeoisie? But, under conditions of capitalism, this happens because capital, property and command of labor and its product, i.e., class rule, is concentrated in the hands of the monopolies and not of the élite itself. Under the new system, command of labor and its product, the national capital, property—all these are concentrated in the hands of the central political bureaucracy alone: apart from it, there is no one who rules production and society. The technocracy does not rule anything and takes no part in decision making. It only carries out the directives of the bureaucracy and supervises the exploitation of the worker, because this is what it is paid to do. The bureaucracy is even willing to pay well, to grant the managers access to the privileges of high consumption, in order to bind them closely to itself and to its system. It does this, however, in its own interest and not in anyone else's. It does not represent, but only bribes the technocrats. From the standpoint of the worker, the expenditure involved in the high consumption level of the managers belongs to that part of the surplus product which is directed against him.

In terms of economic analysis, these expenses are in the unproductive category, since they serve a specific class organization of production and not the process of material production itself.

As LONG AS SOCIAL AND ECONOMIC CONDITIONS permitted, until 1956, the bureaucracy maintained the wages and income of supervisors of hired labor on a comparatively low level, much lower than before the war and considerably lower than at present. Despite the fact that they serve the regime, the consumption of lower officials has been kept within the limits of the workers' subsistence minimum. If they can serve the regime for 1,600 zloty, there is no reason to pay them more. The technocrats serve to realize the class goal of production as its paid and controlled supervisors. Actually, however, their own collective interest is not identical with that of the bureaucracy, but alien and hostile to it. Insofar as the technocrats are outside of bureaucratic control with a possibility of showing their own initiative, they will try to achieve their own goal which is contrary to the goals of production determined by the ruling class.

The whole of these relationships, in other words the system of management, is nothing more than an organizational tool designed to help achieve a specific production goal. Hence in a class society, the whole of management relationships is determined by the class goal of production. This goal is achieved in the production process by the workers and the supervisors of the labor force—the technocrats.

As we have seen, the interest of both these groups is consumption, although it has a different social and material character for each. This means that the class goal of production is opposed to their goals and must be realized against their natural drives. This is the task of the entire system of administration: to force both working masses and the directors of industrial enterprises to achieve the goals indicated by the bureaucracy. For this purpose, the initiative of both these groups must be reduced to a minimum. That is why the management of a factory is deprived of the right to make basic decisions about the factory. It has to carry out the recommendations of the central authority. Decisions about methods, raw materials and costs—what we call administrative decisions—are determined by the central authority. They are transmitted to the factories as obligatory administrative instructions, so-called index "directives." This is the essence of the centralized system of administration which reflects the prevalent conditions of production.

One is often told that the present economic crisis is caused by a faulty system of central administration and that these shortcomings can be overcome by an administrative reform from above. This reasoning mistakes the effect for the cause. A belief that the management system can be changed within existing conditions is obviously utopian.

Can the so-called decentralized system take the place of central management, and be reconciled with the system of production existing in our country? In the decentralized system, a given enterprise is autonomous and basic decisions concerning production are made on the factory level. But decisions are made not by levels, but by people, the social groups which have the monopoly of administration on a given level. An autonomous factory can be administered by any one of two basic groups linked on this level by the organization of production—the working force or the technocrats.

Workers' democracy cannot limit itself to the level of an enterprise. For when economic and political decisions, the actual rule over the surplus product and the labor that creates it, do not belong to the working class, then participation of the workers in managing the enterprise must also become fictitious. Workers' self-rule in an enterprise, therefore, requires full workers' democracy in the state. The working class organized under such conditions will set the goals of social production, guided by its own interest, the interest of the people living today at subsistence level. The goal of production will then be, of course, consumption for the broad masses. This signifies the overthrow of existing production and social relationships and, with them, of the bureaucracy's class rule.

There would be an entirely different situation if the managers and related groups, the technocrats, had a monopoly on autonomous decisions in the factories. Such an arrangement can exist easily behind a facade of a formal workers' government, with a monopolistic government party which, unavoidably, will become a tool for dictatorship over the workers. The old military and political apparatus of power (the political police and the regular army) are, by their very nature, tools of anti-popular democracy. Such a system, which exists today in Yugoslavia, has nothing in common with workers' democracy. There, the working class has no influence on the size, distribution and utilization of the surplus product and its consumption is maintained on a minimum level. Therefore, the worker is again exploited and the production goal is alien to him. Nevertheless, it is not the same goal that exists under the bureaucratic system.

In a so-called decentralized system, an industrial enterprise decides its own production and the achievement of a central plan takes place not by means of administrative measures but through economic actions undertaken from the center (key investments, credit, bank rates, government grants and influence on market prices).

The factory cannot be evaluated, as it is in a centralized system, according to norms established at the top.

The sole possible criterion for evaluating an enterprise is the economic effect of its activity, measured by its profitability, i.e., by the profit it makes in selling its product. This means that the volume, cost, structure and quality of production must be adjusted to demand, so that the newly-created goods can be completely absorbed by the market.

Production is therefore directed at the buyer in the market or—in the last analysis—to the consumer. Since not only industrial consumption goods and labor power are marketed, but also the means of production, production is regulated by the market. As a result, production must be adapted to the needs of consumers, expressed by the demands of the market. The state can modify the market by its economic policy but cannot entirely prevent the consumer from influencing production. The consumer influences production inasmuch as his needs create an effective demand, in proportion to his purchasing power.

Futhermore, in a technocratic system, production for the sake of production, which is the specific class goal of the bureaucracy, cannot be achieved for the following reasons:

a) Production depends on the market and is therefore limited by the volume and structure of consumption much more directly than in a centralized system.

b) In running enterprises, the technocracy tends toward a primary division of income on a broad scale. It is a relatively sizeable stratum and sets aside (like all other privileged groups) the whole of its high individual income for consumption. What follows is a strong demand for high quality and luxury goods and for corresponding services which, of course, exert a significant influence on production.

c) Transforming the technocracy from simple executors of administrative orders and supervisors of hired labor into the "de facto" powers that act at the enterprise level immediately raises its rank and significance in the state. Because of its social function, it is an organized stratum and organized for the management of production at that. It must, therefore, be reckoned with when making economic decisions of a central nature. In this way the "stratum of managers" gains the ability to influence economic decisions which in a centralized system are the monopoly of the central political bureaucracy. Under conditions where production is regulated by the needs of the market and by the economic influence of the state, the influence of the technocracy on income sharing and economic decisions creates a trend toward production designed to satisfy the needs of the high level consumption of the privileged strata. (It is characteristic that the rush to invest going on in Yugoslavia today primarily affects the consumer goods industry.) Hence the so-called decentralized system can in no way be a tool for realizing the class goal of production, associated with the rule of the central political bureaucracy. Also, where the working class continues to be deprived of control over its own labor and its product—that is, where it is exploited—and where the management of enterprises is concentrated in the hands of the technocracy, the decentralized system of management serves to achieve a different production goal. Consequently the membership and character of the ruling class is also different and *production relationships are different*. It follows that a general change in management relationships is possible only in connection with a change in the existing production relationships, while it is impossible within the present framework.

It is production relations, particularly the class goal of production, not an abstractly considered system of management, that determine whether a social-economic system favors economic development or hinders it. As a consequence, they also determine how lasting are the present social relationships and the class rule of the bureaucracy which is based on them.

4.
THE ORIGIN OF THE SYSTEM

ACCORDING TO A VERY widely held theory, the present system in Poland was brought to the country, along with the first governmental team, by the Red Army; it had no economic or social foundations in the "national soil" and could take hold only under conditions where there was an absence of sovereignty. In this way, *the basis* for the bureaucratic system taking hold is transferred beyond the borders of Poland and as such is of not too much interest to the advocates of this view. They are interested in the results, that is, in the existing state of affairs, which is presented as "the Polish raison d'état."

We do not deny that the external conditions under which capitalism was overthrown in our country (weakness of the elements working for an authentic and independent revolution, the decisive role of the Red Army, the strict dependence of the new authorities on the Soviet bureaucracy which had long ago formed itself into a ruling class, and the situation within the international Communist movement), effectively speeded up the process of bureaucratization. We hold, however, that it was objectively conditioned by the level of economic development and the socio-economic structure both of Tsarist Russia and Poland between the wars, as well as of the vast majority of countries in our camp, given the fact of their relative international isolation (the highly developed industrial powers remained capitalist).

When their capitalist systems were abolished, all these countries were backward, with reserves of unused labor, unemployment in the cities and, even more important, overpopulation in the countryside. Their economies were dominated, one way or another, by the capital of industrially developed, imperialist states. Under such conditions, only industrialization can bring a real improvement of material, social and cultural conditions for the mass of people in the cities and countryside.

The apparatus of production in industry was meager and, accordingly, the economic surplus, the basis for accumulation, was very small, too. One could not count on the aid of the capitalist countries. On the contrary, the world market was oriented toward their export of food and raw materials. It subordinated the economies of the under-developed countries to the capital of the industrial powers which domi-nated the market and, thereby, hindered industrialization and perpetu-ated backwardness. The development demanded was independence from the international capitalist markets. Industrialization had to be rapid or not at all. The basis for such a development could be found in large reserves of unused labor. Necessarily, industrialization took place by giving them employment and quickly creating new productive power (a so-called extensive method). However, increased employment could not be accompanied by an equally rapid increase in consumption be-cause this would diminish a still too small economic surplus and make rapid construction of the productive apparatus and further employment impossible. In a word, it would slow down industrialization. It was neces-sary to obtain maximum production and employment while maintaining consumption on a low level—production for production's sake. For a certain time, until a sufficient basis for industry was built, this goal corresponded to the demands of economic development and the general interests of the society.

IN THE COURSE OF INDUSTRIALIZATION, there was a mass migration of available labor from the countryside to the new industries, a rapid nu-merical growth of the working class, the technical and professional intel-ligentsia and a very rapid expansion of the technocratic cadres. At the same time, however, the necessity of limiting consumption dictated a substantial reduction in the earnings of the technocracy, the intelli-gentsia and white-collar employees as compared to the prewar level and a limitation of workers' wages to a very low level, which the old worker cadres felt to be a reduction in wages. Finally, there was a policy of taking away from the peasants all agricultural surpluses over and above the needs of the farm and the peasant's family. The general social interest in industrialization did not correspond with the separate interests of any of the above-mentioned classes and social groups. The natural aspiration of each of these—of the peasants as peasants, the workers as workers, the managers as managers (and not as people who had recently been promoted or who could reasonably hope to improve their lot and status through promotion)—was to increase their individual income to a maximum and improve their material and social situation.

On the other hand, the conditions of industrialization imposed upon them production for the sake of production. For the new authorities, industrialization was a "raison d'être" and a fundamental task. They set about realizing that task despite the differing interests of the remaining classes and social strata and, in a sense, against them: Against the peasantry deprived by force of its surpluses and threatened with loss of property through collectivization; against the working class, whose wages were held down to the lowest possible level and even reduced; against the intelligentsia and the technocracy. The effective realization of such a process of industrialization required that all classes and social strata be deprived of the means of defining their differing interests and fighting for their implementation or in their defense. It required that the whole of political decision-making and of power over the means of production and over the social product be concentrated exclusively in the hands of the new élite. It required, finally, that production be made independent of the regulating influence of the market and that the economic initiative of the working class, of the technocracy and of the peasantry be limited to the greatest possible degree.

It thereby transformed itself into a new ruling class—the central political bureaucracy, while the state which it ruled was transformed in this process into a state of class dictatorship by the bureaucracy. It may be said, therefore, that the nature of the task of industrializing a backward country called to life as a ruling class a bureaucracy which was able to achieve this task, since it alone, through its class interest, represented the interest of industrialization under such conditions—production for the sake of production.

Under these conditions, production relationships based on bureaucratic property insured rapid economic growth, and thanks to this, the remaining classes and social strata, within the bureaucratic system, had real possibilities of improving their lot. Industrialization opened the road to an improved standard of living and a higher material, social and cultural status—a road that led from the countryside into the ranks of the working class, from the ranks of the peasantry and the working class, through the expanding school system at all levels, into the ranks of the technical intelligentsia, the civil service, the liberal professions, the technocracy. Mass social advancement, an end to overpopulation in the countryside and to unemployment were accompanied by an increase in the cultural level of the population in general, by the development of the health services, social benefits, education, etc. Thanks to this and despite coercion and terror, the bureaucracy found enthusiastic support from groups in all social strata. Its power found social support; its ideologists and propagandists could effectively impose its hegemony on society at large, since the achievement of industrialization also meant the realization of a general social interest. The class rule of the bureaucracy was based, therefore, on a solid social foundation and was, therefore, a lasting rule, as long as production relationships—especially the class goal of production—corresponded to the requirements of economic development, in other words, until the foundations of modern industry were built.

5.
ECONOMIC CRISIS OF THE SYSTEM

WE HAVE SEEN THAT the class goal of the bureaucracy—production for production—corresponds to the economic development of the backward country during the period of initial industrialization, that period of building the foundations for industry. How long that period lasts depends on the degree of industrial saturation of the economy achieved in the first stage. In Poland, it ended by the mid-Fifties. In 1956, the apparatus of industrial production was three times larger than in 1949, and in 1960, four times larger.

Let us now look at the situation which develops when—after the fundamental tasks of that period have been accomplished—the class rule of the bureaucracy is maintained and, with it, the same class goal of production. The foundations of a great industry have been built; the investment efforts of the previous years have brought, as a result, a rapid multiplication of resources in the means of production which, in turn, have permitted the employment of the available labor force. Production for the sake of production means a tendency toward a state of affairs in which, possibly, the entire growth in production is confined to Department A, when it assumes the form of new means of production. To maintain this trend in the above-mentioned situation, where the economy is "saturated with industry," means that all production resources, with the exception of what is absolutely indispensable for a minimal growth in consumption, must be used up to create new means of production, to further expand the productive apparatus. The manifold increase in productive resources must be paralleled by a further increase in the part played by capital accumulation in the national income.

The forced industrialization of a backward country cannot take place under conditions of stability. The economic surplus is small and it is not possible to build everything at once while, at the same time, keeping harmonious proportions. Disproportions which arise in the course of rapid expansion of the productive potential create the need for additional investments and additionally swell the investment fund. Let us assume that the whole productive apparatus, multiplied by industrialization, is to be exploited fully; that conditions are to be created for the full utilization of productive resources which have increased many times over. If the trend toward production for the sake of production is maintained, this would require such a tremendous increase in investment that consumption would, as a result, be reduced to a level below that which can be considered minimal from the social point of view. One must remember at the same time that, along with full employment, with the development of an industrial civilization and with an improvement in the general level of social culture, consumption needs also grow which are considered indispensable in these circumstances. To reduce consumption below the subsistence level brings with it the danger—under these conditions—of an economic, social and political catastrophe. It is therefore impossible. Equally impossible is any increase in the level of investment that would create conditions for the full use of the multiplied production resources.

In the final analysis, a low level of social consumption limits production itself in the bureaucratic system as well. This does not happen because of difficulties in marketing the goods produced, but because of the direct limitation of added investment. To maintain production as the goal of production after the foundations of industry have been built (i.e., under conditions of "saturation with industry"), gives rise to *the contradiction between the productive potential of industry in the course of expansion and the low level of consumption.* This contradiction leads to an inability to make full use of increased productive resources, to wastage of the economic surplus and to a slowing down of economic development. Therefore, it becomes the source of a crisis. In the most general terms, the crisis manifests itself in a slowing down of the rate of economic growth despite increased investments designed to expand production.

During the years 1950-1955, the national income grew 74%, about 10% per year. During the years 1956-1960, the national income grew 38%. 6.6% per year. It should also be remembered that this increase was accompanied by a certain fall in the rate of accumulation in the years 1956-1959, as compared to previous pears. However, during 1959-1963, national income increased less than 30% in comparison to 1958—5.2% per year—while at the same time the investment in the national economy grew by 53.4%, by 8.9% yearly, and the industrial investment by 60% (10% per year). The share of accumulation in the national income during the years 1960-1963 was not only higher than 1956-1959 but even higher than 1950-1955, whereas the rate of increase of the national income was almost 50% lower than in the period of the Six Year Plan, 40% lower than in 1956-1959, and 40% lower than planned. (According to the plan the average increase in national income was supposed to reach 8% per year.) This means that with a growing investment one gets a decreased growth rate of the national income. A similar phenomenon can be observed in other countries under bureaucratic dictatorship with a similar share of industry in producing the national income (Czechoslovakia, East Germany, Hungary and probably also the USSR) as was emphasized in the sensational article by a Czech economist, Josef Goldman.

During 1960-1962, the share of material costs in total production grew from 49.7% to 61.9% (in absolute figures an increase of 137.1 billion zloty), while the share of national income decreased from 40.3% to 38.1%. In 1962, the production of the same amount of national income as in 1960 required about 22 billion zloty more in material costs. This indicates the higher costs per unit of produced national income, or a decrease in productive efficiency.

WHAT FACTORS ARE DIRECTLY RESPONSIBLE for slowing down the rate of economic growth and increasing its costs and what are their essential origins?

1) Under conditions in which a trend toward production for the sake of production is accompanied by an expansion in the productive potential, the braking effect of low consumption on economic growth manifests itself most directly in the form of the so-called *inflation barrier*. The rapid growth in investment and employment lead to an expansion of the nominal wage fund; under conditions of production for the sake

of production, supplies of consumer goods reaching the market are not sufficient to meet the growing demand which leads to higher prices and the danger that real wages might fall below the socially acceptable minimum. The inflation barrier is already evident in the present five-year plan period, while in the period 1966-1970, due to an unusually intensive investment program, this same phenomenon will inevitably manifest itself far more sharply.

2) *The raw materials barrier,* the deficit in raw materials and fuels, puts a brake on the possibilities of expanding the manufacturing industries and is one of the reasons why the productive potential is not fully exploited. This is a technical phenomenon which, to all appearances, is not connected with production relationships. In reality, however, two factors inseparably bound up with the present system are at the root of the exceptionally acute shortage of raw materials and fuels. First, the very tendency toward production for the sake of production means that economic growth, where possible, falls in "Department A." In this sector however, material and fuel costs are much higher than in the consumer goods sector. As a result of the one-sided development of the production of the means of production, the consumption of raw materials and fuels per unit of growth of the national income is increased, the share of material costs is increased and the raw materials base is more quickly exhausted. Second, the existing production relationships are—as we shall see—connected with a huge waste of raw materials and fuels.

The consumption of steel for producing the same product is 30% higher in our industry than in the developed countries of Western Europe; the so-called burnings of coal per unit of product are 40-50% higher in our industries than the world average. The plans to lower material production costs are only realized by 50%. This accelerates exhaustion of fuel, raw material base and creates a *raw material barrier.* The only way to overcome it is to invest more in raw materials and fuels which is exceptionally costly and a long range process. At present, such investments represent 45% of all investments in our industry. This contributes to diminishing national income and increasing basic costs.

3) *Squandering of the economic surplus* in the form of excessive consumption of raw materials and fuels, inability to make full use of the productive potential and immoderate increase in reserves. We have already spoken about the waste of raw materials. The degree to which the productive potential on an industry-wide scale is made use of is not known to anyone and research in this area is complicated by the fact that enterprises seek to conceal their reserves. In the electromechanical industry, the degree of utilization of the productive potential is reckoned

at 58 per cent of capacity. Full use of productive capacity in this one branch of industry only would increase the national income by 18 billion zloty yearly. Failure to make full use of the productive apparatus is widespread; for instance, building machines in all the construction enterprises in the country are used at only about 20% of capacity. Rejects ("Buble") for which there is no demand or which cannot be marketed because of poor quality, make for an excessive increase in reserves.

This production represents a loss. Its costs produce no new values or new consumer goods. In 1961-1963, the national economy lost about 21 billion zloty. The amount of unnecessary stocks included in the plan itself is not known; at any rate, the increase of stores and reserves in 1960 absorbed 28.2 billion zloty (7.4% of the national income) and in 1961, 32.9 billion zloty (8.1% of the national income) and in 1962, 21.4 billion zloty (5.1% of the national income) and in 1963, 32.3 billion zloty (7.3% of the national income).

The common cause of non-utilization of productive capacity and of accumulation of unneeded reserves is *the general inadaptation of production to needs.* The mass production of lines of goods which can find no market and which are dispatched to swelling warehouses is accompanied, not only by a sharp deficit in raw materials, but also by a shortage of certain types of tools and equipment leading to numerous work interruptions, non-utilization of productive resources and a general lack of rhythm in production (catching up with plans toward the end of the reporting period at the cost of excessive effort on the part of the worker and of lowered quality of goods). Production is not adapted to needs. This is true not only in the structure of the various lines of goods, but also so far as quality is concerned. The poor quality of raw materials and tools contribute to lowering the quality of the end product and speeds up the wear on the means of production, a source of additional waste. It is hard to sum up the excessive use of raw materials and fuels, the non-utilization of capacity, the unnecessary stocks and the damages arising from poor quality production. There is no doubt, however, that all this waste consumes many tens of billions of zloty yearly. Compared to this waste, all economic scandals put together seem quite insignificant.

4) *The non-utilization of so-called intensive factors of economic growth,* that is of increased productivity through modernization, technical progress, technological progress (product improvement, reduction in raw material costs, etc.) and organizational progress (discovery and exploitation of reserves). The achievement of the stage of "saturation with industry" means that the productive apparatus has been expanded to the point

where employment of the available labor force at a given level of productivity in agriculture is assured. Further growth cannot take place simply by expanding the productive apparatus and employing labor reserves, i.e., by extensive means, but must be based mainly on factors which lead to increased productivity, i.e., intensive factors.

According to the figures published in the Fall of 1962 by the Minister of Internal Trade, the objectives of the 5-year plan in the area of new products were achieved by 57%, in the area of mechanization by 44%, in automation by 28%; and the tendency of various industrial enterprises not to disclose all their reserves is generally known. Failures in the area of increasing labor efficiency when the development cannot, as previously, rely on extensive factors, contribute to further decreases in the growth rate of the national income.

5) *The export barrier,* that is, difficulties in the foreign trade balance of payments due to increased imports from the capitalist countries and the inability of the manufacturing industry to export. Eighteen per cent of production in the engineering industry is destined for export; of this, however, export to capitalist markets amounts only to four per cent and export to the highly developed Western countries to only one per cent, while exchanges with those countries constitute about 39 per cent of Poland's entire foreign trade and the balance of payments in this sector is in very serious straits. This is connected with the non-fulfillment by industry of export production plans and with the low technical and qualitative levels of home industry production. Due to poor quality or to excessive raw material costs, these goods find no buyers or are sold at a disadvantageous ratio of export production costs to the price of goods purchased abroad. Shortcomings in industrial exports are patched up with increased raw material, fuel and food exports and this is the least profitable kind of export. In this way, the national income to be shared is decreased, while at the same time the internal deficit in raw materials and fuels (the raw materials barrier) and the shortage of food articles on the home market (the inflation barrier) are increased.

The *symptoms* of economic crisis enumerated in Points 3, 4 and 5 follow essentially from the same causes and we will analyze them jointly. These causes are often sought in the defective functioning of the economy, shortcomings in the system of incentives and indices, in the system of management. Enterprises are interested in fulfilling directive indices or, to be more precise, the basic index, in which the total planned production is contained. Given strict bank control of the wage fund, fulfillment of this target is achieved most easily by turning out lines of goods whose prices are fixed substantially above costs and which are characterized by a large participation of material costs and a low participation of labor in the final product.

Managements try to produce that which assures the easy fulfillment of the plan and not that which is necessary. They try to conceal their reserves in order to be assigned reduced tasks in the plan. It is easiest to fulfill the plan when it has been set below the productive capacity of the enterprise (i.e., when the reserves have not been taken into account) and when one turns out mainly those products whose prices are fixed substantially above production costs (which therefore assure a high rate of accumulation) or by selecting lines of goods which have a high value but take little labor to produce, i.e., lines of goods which consume a large amount of raw materials. Improved quality, reduced material costs, technological progress, everything that increases the participation of human labor and decreases the value of the raw material in the end product, all this renders more difficult the fulfillment of the quantitative total production plan. Modernization and increased efficiency achieved by the enterprise through its own means give rise to the danger that the wage fund index will be exceeded or that the quantitative plan will not be fulfilled. Therefore, the squandering of raw materials, the lack of adaptation of production to needs, low quality of production, difficulties in achieving technical progress, the flight from production for export and the negligible effect of industrial exports. According to some, the fault lies with the total production index which acts as a counter-incentive. According to others, it lies with the centralized system of management which not only creates counter-incentives but also paralyzes the initiative of both the managers and the workers and, at the same time, the intensive factors of economic growth.

WE HAVE SEEN THAT the centralized system of management is a function of the prevailing relations of production and cannot be altered in a general sense within the framework of those relationships. Let us now see whether the sources of the above-mentioned crisis symptoms do not lie deeper and whether a reform of the indices within the framework of prevailing production relationships will permit us to overcome the crisis.

First of all, it is not true that managers' and workers' teams are entirely deprived of initiative and do not show any. It is impossible to make central decisions on everything, still more difficult to control the execution of all specific orders and even of all directives. This means that managers as well as workers, act partially on their own initiative. It is impossible to evaluate an enterprise from twenty points of view simultaneously. The worker tries to lower efficiency and hides the reserves in his sector to delay the change in norms; he makes a product of inferior quality in order to meet the norm more easily. The manager will ignore the poor product because of the "factory's interest," i.e., production of quantity instead of quality. The management hides reserves in order to obtain lower plan figures, chooses high accumulation or material-consuming assortments to carry out the plan more easily, tries to escape production of labor consuming export goods and to avoid technological progress, improvement or modernization achieved at the expense of the enterprise. All this massive social initiative, apparently directed toward the execution of plans decreed by the bureaucracy, is in fact directed against them, and therefore directed against the class goal of production. Like all social initiative, it is a conscious activity to realize the aims and interests of the people concerned. The technocrats claim to act in the so-called interest of the enterprise (which is really their own interest) and also in the name of a "compromise" with the workers which would enable both to arrange themselves within the existing framework of production and administration.

In fact, what we have here is not a contradiction between the objectives of the plan and the anti-stimuli resulting from faulty directives, but a contradiction between the class goal of the ruling bureaucracy (production for production) and the interests of basic groups who achieve the production (maximum consumption). In other words, it is a contradiction between the class goal of production and consumption, and it results from existing conditions, not from mismanagement.

This contradiction is inseparable from the existing conditions of production and has accompanied them from the beginning. But in the stage of primitive industrialization the first task consisted of building the foundations of industry and employing available labor—therefore production for production, and an extensive development. Almost every new enterprise which increased the productive apparatus was an achievement. In that stage, the system was increasing economic development and its contradictions were of secondary importance. After the productive apparatus had been developed and labor reserves absorbed by industry, the main problem was how to use productively the potential created, and how to increase labor efficiency. Then, the non-adjustment of production to needs, the low quality, brakes on technological and organizational progress, in other words, the paralysis of intensive factors of economic growth became of major significance in hampering growth. And the disproportions of the system became most striking when the *contradiction between the developed productive potential and the low level of social consumption became evident.* It is precisely this contradiction which causes the crisis with all its symptoms. Without eliminating it, without changing the goal of production and the conditions of production as a whole, it will be impossible to overcome the ever growing crisis.

There are proposals to change the chief index from gross production to net production and more far-reaching proposals to accept profit and loss as the chief index. What can such reforms bring about in present conditions of administering production? Probably a less wasteful use of fuel and raw materials. But the basic contradictions will not be eliminated. The enterprise will still hide its reserves to achieve a lower and more easily attainable basic index; will still choose assortments with a high accumulation rate which will make it easier to achieve the plan figure and carry out the directive which is always expressed in quantities. There will still be an assortment of goods of a quality not fitted to the needs, with the usual consequences for our foreign trade. The adaptation of production to needs can be made only by the market buyer —and ultimately by the consumer—but never by the central planner who fixes the price of goods by himself and without reference to the market and who judges an enterprise by its execution of central directive indices which are necessarily expressed by quantities. Technological progress, modernization and improvements achieved by the enterprise from its own resources are contrary to the interests of the central planner so that the brakes on technological and organizational progress, i.e., on the intensive factors of growth, will not be eliminated.

That is why the symptoms of crisis described in points 3, 4 and 5 (waste of economic surpluses, non-utilization of intensive factors and the export barrier) are also derived from the conditions of production and cannot be overcome within their framework. Let us accept, for the moment, the abstract assumption that bureaucracy could achieve this. If the existing economic conditions, i.e., production for production, are preserved, the crisis would take the form described at the beginning of this section. The whole wasted part of the economic surplus would be turned into additional means of production whose utilization in accordance with the class goal of production would require an increase in accumulation and the reduction of consumption below the socially necessary level. In practice, the inflation barrier would move into the foreground. It would make it impossible to raise investment, to utilize the additional means of production. The crisis would then be reduced to its essence, the contradiction between a high production potential and a low level of consumption. It can thus be seen that the waste of economic surplus, the non-utilization of growth factors, etc., are only

manifestations and camouflaged forms of this basic contradiction Therefore no improvement in the functioning of the economy, even if it were
possible, would overcome the crisis, unless it were linked to a change in
the class goal of production for consumption.

Do any serious economic reserves exist today that would help to alle-
viate the crisis, at least temporarily?

Such reserves existed in the mid-Fifties when the basic industrialization was achieved. The contradiction between the high production potential (three times that of 1949) and the low level of consumption became manifest, and the economic crisis started. The fundamental source
of the reserves was the fact that investments made previously began
to produce profits. There was therefore a chance to achieve a relatively
high increase of the national income with a lower share of accumulation
and a higher share of consumption.

Another essential source of reserves, particularly relevant for possibilities of increased consumption, was agriculture. Industrialization
caused the transfer of many superfluous workers from agriculture to
non-agricultural employment in urban centers, thereby reducing over-
population of the countryside, improving the agrarian structure and increasing the income of the majority of farms. This created a possibility
of developing agricultural proficiency and increasing the quantity of
farm produce. Under the Stalinist policy of ruthlessly depriving the
peasant of all surpluses and the constant threat of collectivization, such
possibilities did not exist since, for a peasant, it did not pay to increase
his production. The change in agricultural policy based on the abandon-
ment of forced collectivization and the creation of conditions to make
farming profitable by easing the requisition of surpluses, on concessions to the peasants, could in that situation mobilize the reserves
without a considerable government investment and without a radical
change in peasant economy.

As can be observed, in both cases the mobilization of reserves represented a possibility of increased consumption, although from the point
of view of the bureaucracy it was only a retreat, a necessary evil with a
view to maintaining power and class rule during the critical social and
economic conditions of those stormy years. The political spring for mo-
bilizing the reserves was the general revolt against the Stalinist forms of
dictatorship and, primarily, the pressure of the working class which
caused an increase of 30% in real wages, a change in agrarian policy and
a parallel increase in peasant income.

The concessions to increased consumption made the continuing contradictions between the developed productive potential and low level of social consumption less marked, at any rate, temporarily. And this was the main cause of the improved economic situation in 1956-1959. As we see it, however, the reserves permitting the increased consumption belonged to the earlier period of forced industrialization. During the subsequent period of crisis the system did not produce any new reserves and the remaining ones, after the years of the glorious youth of the system, were naturally exhausted.

Toward the end of the Five Year Plan (1956-1960) the productive powers organized during the early period were fully mobilized; further growth called for greater increase of labor efficiency or another increase of investments. At the same time, more or less, the rural economy reached the ceiling of its production under the given technical conditions and the rate of exploitation of the state. In 1956-1958, rural production grew by 15%, and in 1959-1960, by only 5%. Today, it hardly catches up with the population increase. Stagnation in agricultural production became a barrier to increasing consumption, and in order permanently to end the economic crisis it would be necessary to produce a radical change in the proportions of investment and economic growth to achieve modernization and a renovation of the technological base of agriculture along with the steady, rapid growth of the industrial production of consumers goods. This, however, would mean to change the goal of production.

Meanwhile, during the class struggle of 1956-1957, the bureaucracy had kept its political power and, in 1958-59, achieved a stabilized class dictatorship. The conditions of production that guaranteed its rule were maintained together with the class goal of production. Under such circumstances, nobody will be surprised that, at the threshhold of the present Five Year Plan, the economic crisis had reached a ripe phase. The system does not have, today, any considerable reserves and its difficulties do not result any longer from the Stalinist agrarian policy or the necessity of quickly building an armaments industry. The economic crisis can be reduced in its pure form to the crisis within existing production conditions. There are no possibilities, therefore, that it will recede; on the contrary, with the further development of production for production, the contradiction between the developed productive potential and low consumption will become more acute and so will the crisis.

The investment program for 1966-1970, anticipates creating 1.5 million new jobs for the "demographic surplus" (for full employment there should be even more), while the investment expenditure is supposed to reach about 830-840 billion zloty. This means a further increase in the share of investment in the national income by some 20%. In spite of such huge expenditures, the planned increase of the national income is supposed to be 30% during the five years. This shows that even at the planning stage, the bureaucracy takes the braking action of the system into consideration. It appears from the Report of the Central Committee of the PUWP at the IVth Party Congress that the plan is based on stabilized real wages. In other words, the size of accumulation funds is fixed directly on the edge of the inflation barrier. But we know from experience that the realization of the investment program will require much higher investments than planned. It means that the inflation barrier will be crossed so that the real wages will be pushed below the minimum level socially necessary, or the plan will not be executed. In that case, the growth of national income will be stopped again and unemployment drastically increased. (We recall for comparative purposes that in the period of the Six Year Plan, with investments of less than 319 billion zloty at 1962 prices, employment rose by 2.4 million and national income increased by 70% as compared to 1949.) In both cases, the economic crisis will be unavoidably strengthened.

Therefore, no justification for the functioning of the economy, even were it possible, can lead to overcoming the crisis if it does not involve a change of the class goal of production and a shift over to production for the sake of consumption.

Production relations based on bureaucratic ownership have become chains hampering the country's productive forces; with every day this continues, the crisis deepens. Therefore, the solution of the economic crisis requires the overthrow of these production relations and the elimination of the class rule of the bureaucracy.

6.
RELATIONS OF PRODUCTION IN AGRICULTURE AND THE CRISIS

The production relationships in our agriculture are based on individual peasant ownership and on a state monopoly of the market. (The state is, in practice, the exclusive supplier of industrial goods for the needs of the countryside and the purchaser of the major part of the peasants' produce.) In 1961, agricultural produce amounted to about 60.8 % of the end product of individual farms (by end product we mean that part of the total product which remains after subtracting material costs). Taking into account the fact that a peasant's farm is also a family unit which produces its own livelihood, its ties with the market are very close ones. This may result from two fundamentally different causes. Either we have to do with a specialized, rationally run and efficient agricultural enterprise, producing for the market while the family's consumption needs are met by the market; or else the farm is at a low level of development at the same time that an unfavorable ratio of prices between industrial goods and agricultural produce, and fiscal oppression compel the family to limit its own consumption if it wishes to maintain its farm.

According to official data concerning the IER (category of farms on a higher level than average), consumption of food commodities and clothing in a peasant's family is growing steadily, as the farm area grows. Various farm sizes show relatively small differences in expenditures for other consumers goods. But if we look separately at the consumption of meat, the difference becomes striking. In 1961-62, the annual consumption of meat per person in the farm category of up to 3 hectares (44.6% of all farms) was 26.2 kilograms; in the category 3-7 hectares (28.9% of all farms), it was 27.7 kg.; in the category 7-10 hectares (12.7% of all farms), it was 34.3 kg.; in the category 10-15 hectares (7.9% of all farms), it was 39.3 kg.; and in the category above 15 hectares (2.8% of all farms), it was 46.6 kg.

It should be remembered that Norm A (hardly sufficient) indicates 37 kg. of meat and meat products per person. Therefore, over 85% of peasants—main producers of meat—consume meat below the physically hardly sufficient norm. No wonder that a rise in income immediately means the greater consumption of meat.

Next to meat, the food which shows marked consumption changes in relation to income is potatoes. Generally, the consumption of potatoes decreases with a higher standard of living. But in peasants' families it is the opposite. In 1961-62, consumption of potatoes per member of the peasant's family on farms below 3 hectares amounted to 216 kg.; on farms from 3-7 hectares—217 kg.; from 7-10 hectares—239 kg.; from 10-15 hectares—251 kg.; above 15 hectares—269 kg.

From the figures quoted above, it follows that, from the point of view of the peasant, a high degree of involvement with the market is not a means to maximize consumption but—on the contrary—is achieved *at the price of limiting the basic consumption of the peasant family.*

What compels the peasant family to limit personal consumption so sharply? First, direct *fiscal pressure*, that is taxes and compulsory deliveries. True, compulsory deliveries are paid for, but at rates which are, on the average, only one half of free market prices. In 1961, farms which conduct agricultural bookkeeping received for compulsory deliveries 7% of their total income for produce, which means that the state took over for nothing, in the form of compulsory deliveries, 7% of the produce of an average farm. In the same year, taxes swallowed up 7.5% of the income from produce of the average peasant farm.

Second, the pressure exerted through *the state monopoly of the market.* The state is the only *supplier* of everything that the peasant farm acquires on the market. It is also the purchaser. In 1961, 76% of the income from produce of the average peasant farm came from the sale of produce to the state (of this, seven per cent was for compulsory deliveries). Apart from compulsory deliveries, the state acquires from the peasants their produce within the framework of the system of above-norm contracting and purchase at prices which are on the average 30 % below free market prices.

What forces the peasant to sell "voluntarily" to the state a major part of his produce on such unfavorable terms? In some areas, above-norm contracting and purchase are the only available form of marketing. But a decisive role is played by another factor: the pressure exerted by the state as the monopolistic supplier of all non-agricultural goods indispensable for the farm and the peasant family. Only contracting farms have the right to buy coal, which is indispensable for livestock breeding (and is the source of over 69% of the income from produce of the average peasant farm) and artificial fertilizer.

Through the state market monopoly, the ruling bureaucracy artificially opens the so-called *price scissors* and drains the production surplus from the countryside. Much is written about the prewar price fork, the relationship of prices for industrial goods and agricultural produce, unfavorable to the countryside.

Let us compare the prices of certain industrial articles bought by the peasants during the years 1927-28 and in 1962, counting in Kilograms of rye. For a one-furrow plough in 1927-28, the peasant paid 100 kg. of rye; now he pays 112 kg. of rye, if we count in terms of the prices of the contracts and non-obligatory supplies which form 69% of goods income of the average farm; or 73.3 kg. of rye in free market prices (24% of goods income). For a given quantity of coal he paid, before the war, 36 kg. of rye; today he pays 53 kg. in terms of non-obligatory supplies and 36 kg. at free market prices.

In comparison with 1928, the industrial potential has grown six times, industrial efficiency has increased and industrial costs of production have decreased much more than they have in agriculture. The artificial maintainance of agricultural prices on such a low level constitutes the main tool for helping the system to obtain farm products—not by increasing farm production but by decreasing the consumption of the rural population and resisting investments on the farms.

Where does such a tendency come from?

We have seen in Chapter II that the purchase of food from the peasants is, from the bureaucracy's point of view, a constituent part of expenditure for the purchase of labor for the industrial and service sectors. We have also seen that production for the sake of consumption (which agricultural production is by its very nature) is, from the bureaucracy's point of view a necessary evil, while production for the sake of production is its goal. In terms of achieving that class goal, the size of agricultural production is determined by the level of employment and the minimum for existence. It is not therefore a question of maximum development of that production, but rather of obtaining at minimum cost the food necessary to feed the labor force employed in industry, construction, transport and services. The system of draining surpluses by reducing the market prices of produce from individual peasant farms (and, accordingly, limiting the consumption and investment power of rural population) is therefore a means of reducing expenditure for the purchase of labor power and results from the class goal of production. In this way, the exploitation of the peasant is a result of the exploitation of the worker and is inseparably bound to production relationships prevailing in industry.

THE SYSTEM OF DRAINING away surpluses deprives the countryside of a material base for the expansion of its own productive potential. This leads to a relative stagnation of agricultural production with a simultaneous rapid growth of production resources in industry. In this way, a disproportion rapidly appears, known officially as "the inability of agriculture to keep up with industry." This phenomenon is common to industrialized countries ruled by bureaucratic dictatorships and is in reality an essential element in the contradiction between the expanded productive potential and the low level of social consumption. Despite this fact, the standard of living of the rural population is much higher today than it was before the war. General productivity in agriculture has also increased, especially productivity per worker. This is the result of industrialization which liberated the countryside of the chief economic scourge of prewar days: millions of redundant workers went to the towns or at least found employment and wages outside agriculture. This happened in the period 1949-1955; yet the agricultural policy of that period, consisting in deprivation of surpluses by force and in threats of expropriation by collectivization, made it impossible to take advantage of the possibilities created by the elimination of over-population for increasing agricultural production and peasant consumption.

In 1956, the policy of collectivization was given up and the system of draining the resources of the countryside was changed: economic coercion exerted through the state market monopoly and through the price scissors took the place of administrative and police coercion. This definite concession, forced on the authorities though it was, allowed the countryside to take advantage of the reserves created by the elimination of over-population in order to increase agricultural production and its own consumption. But the nature of the relationships between the peasant producers and the state did not change. They still amount to a drainage of production surpluses and to achieving the indispensable supply of produce, not through the expansion of agriculture, but by limiting the consumption of the peasant family and its possibilities of investment—though all this is done by different methods than were used before. It could hardly be otherwise, since the old production relationships in industry have been maintained. That is why the growth of agricultural production was bound to come to a halt, as indeed it did when the reserves created during the Six Year Plan were exhausted.

During 1956-60, total agricultural production grew by 20%, but three-quarters of this increase belongs to the period 1956-58. In recent years, 1961-64, farm production hardly matches the population increase, and its periodic fluctuations are in the category of economic cataclysms. What we have here is stagnation. But today, unlike the period 1949-55, no new reserves are growing which might later become the foundation for rapid progress; the plan for 1966-70, anticipates maintaining present employment on the individually owned farms, with certain decreases in the area of peasants' property.

The source of stagnation today is no longer any so-called "inappropriate agricultural policy," any specific *form* of drainage of the resources of the countryside, but the *system itself* of draining surpluses, by which the countryside is deprived of the material basis of its own development. (The Fund for the Development of Agriculture does not change this fact: for instance to plough one hectare with a tractor belonging to an Agricultural Circle costs, at the official rate, 220 zloty, 100 kilograms of rye at above-norm contracting prices, the equivalent of a one-share plough. For the majority of villages, mechanization in this way is too expensive: in the period 1959-1962, the fund's facilities were utilized at the rate of about 22%.) In other words the crisis in agriculture results today directly from *existing production relationships.*

What are the prospects for the future? To answer this question we must consider a factor not considered thus far in our discussion of the relationship between peasant production and the state, namely, the internal structure of agricultural property. In 1960, small farms (0.5—5 hectares) represented 52.5% of the total number (and the "dwarf farms" under 3 hectares—over 40%), and occupied 27.5% of the cultivated land. Farms averaging 10 hectares constituted 10.7% of the total, and occupied 32.6% of the cultivated land.

Per 100 small farms there are 97.5 heads of cattle and 23.3 horses, where per 100 farms above 15 hectares, there are 590 heads of cattle and 216.2 horses. Aside from that, 100 (exclusively larger IER) farms investigated in 1962 owned 98 private tractors. All these figures indicate a tendency toward the development of capitalist farming conditions in agriculture. Meanwhile, the process of property polarization is unusually slow and hired labor plays only a small part: ony 3% of the farms constantly use hired labor (300 man-days per year or more).

The conditions of capitalization are that: 1) the largest farms should have sufficient means of accumulation, 2) there should be a large supply of cheap land created by failing dwarf holdings and 3) there should be a large supply of cheap labor in the countryside.

In the period 1950-1955, the main forms of exploitation of the countryside were compulsory deliveries and taxes, burdens growing progressively in proportion to the size of the farm. Together with the anti-kulak policy, this deprived the largest farms of the means of capital accumulation and even led to their downfall. After 1956, the main form of exploitation became the price scissors, applied thanks to the state's monopoly of the market. This is a form of exploitation which weighs equally on all producers, therefore it is relatively easier on the richest farms which, at the same time, gain the means of accumulation and it is hardest on the poorest farms. If the mass of dwarf holdings (52.5% of the total) were then deprived of sources of income outside agriculture, under conditions of a wide-spread price scissors, they could not stand up to the fiscal pressure and would have to fail. As a result, a large supply of cheap labor and cheap land, needed for capitalization, would be created.

What saves the mass of small holdings from failure and puts a brake on the process of capitalization in agriculture is the employment of peasants in state enterprises. The so-called peasant-workers constitute about 26% of all persons employed in the socialized economy, while the holdings of peasant-workers make up 45.5% of the sum total of individual farms in our country. By employing in industry people who live in the countryside and have small land holdings, the labor surplus has been eliminated to a large degree.

In recent years, reductions in the factories showed that first to be fired are the peasant-workers. At the same time, and for the first time since 1945, the rate of wages in agriculture dropped by 15% in 1962.

The investment program for 1966-70, foresees creating 1.5 million new working posts. But even if successfully carried out, it will not cover the increase of the working-age population. Under conditions of un-employment and strong pressures on the labor market it can be forecast easily that the available working posts will go to inhabitants of indus-trial areas, while the peasant-workers will be fired. Therefore, it is not realistic to expect the same level of employment in individual farming, even if the plan is successful. But this is unlikely to happen, because the investment fund of the plan will, as usual, be insufficient for a sensible investment program. Yet, it is calculated at the verge of the inflation barrier, so that any excess expenditure may have serious con-sequences. The prospect of an insufficient investment means a serious rise in unemployment and, in particular, mass firings of peasant-workers.

As we have already seen, a high percentage of peasant-workers is an essential factor in fighting rural overpopulation, in maintaining the existence of small farms and the main obstacle to further capitalization. An unavoidable consequence of the progressing industrial crisis will be the reappearance of a rural labor surplus (through reduction of the number of peasant-workers in the factories) and the collapse of many small farms. With the resulting overpopulation, conditions will emerge which will contribute to the transformation of the richest peasant prop-erties into capitalist farms.

The crisis in agriculture is closely connected with the economic crisis in industry and—within the framework of prevailing production relationships—can only go from bad to worse. To overcome the crisis in agriculture, as in the entire economy, it is necessary to overthrow the existing production relationships inhering in bureaucratic class rule.

7.
THE FIRST ANTI-BUREAUCRATIC REVOLUTION, 1956-1957

Our paper was to include a chapter devoted to an analysis of the class struggle in the years 1956-1957. Due to the intervention of the Ministry of the Interior, we did not have time to write that chapter. However, since it is essential from the point of view of understanding our political standpoint and also because attempts at evaluating the events of October (the causes of the failure of the left wing current and the fiasco of the 1956 revolution became the starting point for the evolution of our views), it is necessary to summarize that chapter.

The Fifties produced an international crisis for Stalinism—the first phase of a general crisis of the bureaucratic dictatorship. It resulted in the first revolutionary acts of the working class: the general strike in the GDR and the demonstrations and street fighting of June 17, 1953, in Berlin, the series of strikes in the concentration camps in the USSR, the events of June 1956 in Poznan and the first anti-bureaucratic revolutions in Poland and in Hungary.

The economic background to these upheavels is provided by an understanding of the economic crisis of the system. Once the foundations of industry had been built and labor surplus employed, the contradiction between the expanded productive potential and the low level of social consumption became obvious. For the vast majority of people, the prospects for improved living conditions were no longer connected with mass transition from the lower classes to strata with a better material and social situation. Instead, they were concerned with improved material, social and cultural conditions of living in their own stratum. The distinct class interest of the peasants, forcibly deprived of their surpluses, of the workers receiving starvation wages, of the supervisors of hired labor, relatively badly paid and deprived of the right to make decisions, necessitated increased consumption which was contrary to the class goal of production set by the bureaucracy.

Once these distinct class interests assumed decisive significance in economic and social practice and in people's awareness, the whole of society found itself in conflict with the ruling bureaucracy. The Stalinist system of total police dictatorship which deprived all classes and social strata of the means of struggling for their own specific interests became the object of universal hatred. This form of dictatorship thereby lost its effectiveness as a bureaucratic tool. There followed the 20th Congress.

Since the social crisis erupted in the opening phase of the system's economic crisis, the economy still had substantial reserves, created during the initial period of industrialization. These were reserves for increased consumption released when the state power felt threatened by the pressure exerted directly by the working class. But the very fact that these reserves existed also created the possibility of a transient stabilization, the economic basis for an external reform of the system—and means of maintaing the class rule of the bureaucracy.

The Hungarian bureaucracy was saved by the revolution's isolation and by armed Russian intervention. How could Poland's bureaucracy retain power by peaceful means?

The fate of a revolution is decided by the clash of two fundamental social classes: the working class and the bureaucracy. The Poznan events showed clearly enough that these are the main forces in the conflict and that the revolution requires the leadership of the working class as the logical and most consistent anti-bureaucratic force.

In order that the working class have the ability to play the leading role, it must be conscious of its distinct, particular interests. It must express them in the form of a political program and organize itself—as a class fighting for power—into its own political party or parties.

The so-called October Left—a political current made up in large measure of the natural leaders of working class, youth and intellectual opinion—could have been a substitute for the political vanguard of the mass working class movement. The October Left differed from the liberal current, especially in its views on the Workers' Councils, in which it saw the basis for new production relationships and the nucleus of a new political power. But it was not a uniform movement. The Left did not separate itself from the technocratic current in the Workers' Council movement (the demand that factories be run by the Councils did not go beyond the program of the technocracy) nor from the liberal bureaucracy, in the political showdown on a national scale. It did not set itself apart from the general anti-Stalinist front as a specifically proletarian movement. In this situation, it was evidently unable to formulate its own political program, to propagate it in an organized manner among the masses, to create a party. Without all this, it could not become a politically independent force, and therefore, it had to transform itself into a leftist appendage of the ruling liberal bureaucracy.

The Eighth Plenum of the CC of the PUWP was a victory of the liberal wing within the bureaucracy. This wing aimed at mitigating the social crisis and stabilizing the system by internal reform, economic concessions and by achieving hegemony; it aimed at taking the lead in the mass movement in order to contain it within limits safe for the system. A leadership was chosen which enjoyed popularity and a platform of reforms and promises indispensable for the realization of the liberal bureaucracy's aims was put forward. Giving up collectivization and changing the agricultural policy met the demands of the entire country-side (though it most benefited the rich peasantry) ; widening the margin of private initiative corresponded to the aspirations of the petty bourgeoisie; the accord with the Episcopate removed an important factor of political tension and created new political-propaganda possibilities (the electoral pact with Wyszynski); the consistent post-October policy of increasing the salaries and incomes of managers aimed at associating the technocracy with the system; criticism of the Six Year Plan and the announcement of a new economic policy gave rise to universal hopes for an improved standard of living. Above all, however, the national question brought popularity to the new leadership: the masses tended to regard the newly-won sovereignty of the Polish bureaucracy as their own. On the other hand, the working class was not even promised the wage increases that were later won. The *fait accompli* of the creation of Workers' Councils in the factories was recognized, but they were given no real rights and the new leadership of the bureaucracy, first secretly and later openly, opposed their development.

October 1956 was, however, not only the month of the Eighth Plenum, but also the climax of the revolution. In the immediate post-October months, the new leadership of the bureaucracy was completely deprived of the means of crushing the revolution by force. The only chance it had of retaining power was through the mobilization of confidence in, and authority for, the new leadership. It had to win hegemony over the masses, make concessions and maneuver till such time as economic stabilization would lessen the tension of the social crisis and the apparatus of power would regain its repressive strength and control over society. The only chance of expanding the revolution was to propose a working class program and to organize a movement around it opposed to the rule of the liberal bureaucracy. At this decisive moment, the Left not only failed to put forward such a program and organize itself into a party, but it lent support to the liberal bureaucracy, the chief anti-revolutionary force. All the great authority which the activists of the Left enjoyed in their arenas was passed on to the new leadership. In this way, the Left contributed to maintaining the power of the bureaucracy, and by the same token, it prepared its own political death and the defeat of the revolution. In the spring of 1957, at the Ninth Plenum, the leadership of the bureaucracy was able to declare a "struggle on two fronts" aimed at restoring the monolitic unity of the Party and able openly to condemn the concept of expanding the Workers' Councils and convoking a national congress of councils as an "anarchistic Utopia." By the autumn of 1957, the bureaucracy was able to enter a decisive battle. It began with the police crushing a strike by streetcar workers in Lodz, then came the closing of *Po Prostu*, dispersing mass demonstrations in the streets of Warsaw (October 4-7, 1957), abolishing freedom of the press, a purge in the Party which did away with freedom of discussion within the PUWP and restored its monolithic character and, finally, in the spring of 1958, the subordination of the moribund Workers' Councils to the control of the Party apparatus directly through the Plant Committees and indirectly through the trade union apparatus (the creation of the so-called Workers' Self-Government Conference). In this way, all the achievements of October which exceeded the framework of an internal reform of the system were liquidated and the October Left was finally crushed.

The mobilization of economic reserves and an increase in real wages, fought for and won by the working class, created a base for the stabilization of a reformed bureaucratic dictatorship. As we have seen, however, these stabilizing reserves were of a transient nature; production relationships were not altered, and so, with the exhaustion of these reserves toward the end of the last five-year plan, the economic crisis appeared in a more mature form. The system no longer possesses economic reserves nor any margin for further reforms: those reforms which do not involve the class nature of the system have already been carried out. With the renewal of the economic crisis, a general social crisis has erupted.

8.
THE GENERAL SOCIAL CRISIS OF THE SYSTEM

No SOCIAL SYSTEM HAS COLLAPSED solely because it exploited and oppressed the masses. On the other hand, no class can maintain its rule for any length time if it is based only on coercion, victimizing the rest of society.

To achieve some minimal viability, a ruling class must provide other classes and strata, within the framework of its system, improved material and spiritual conditions of life, the basis of which is economic development. If it cannot do that, even bayonets will not help. Thus, as long as the conditions of production underlying the class rule of the central political bureaucracy favored rapid economic development (the period of forced industrialization), mass social advancement improved the lot of millions of people and raised the cultural level of society as a whole, the bureaucracy could establish its hegemony. And during the post-October [1957] period of stabilization, although social mobility was limited, the working class and almost all social strata, nevertheless, saw a tangible increase in their individual incomes. But what can the bureaucracy give them, today, when the system is in economic crisis?

In the nature of things, the working class is the chief opponent of the bureaucracy. The worker stands on the lowest level of the social hierarchy with everyone from the foreman to the prime minister above him and no one below him. Because the exploitation of the worker constitutes the material basis maintaining the system, the entire apparatus of power and coercion is directed primarily against the working class. This is the way it was and the way it is now. But in the periods 1949-1955 and 1956-1959, the workers' lot improved, though for different reasons in each of these two periods. However, according to official statistical data, which we have already cited, in the 1960-1963 period the average real income per capita among families of industrial workers only rose by 2.6% (0.6% yearly on the average). Taking into account the hidden increase in living costs due to changes in lines of goods and, in recent years, the price rise of articles of prime necessity, the standard of living of the working class has actually declined during the last four years. This state of affairs was particularly painful for the majority of families where no one advanced and the number of wage earners did not increase.

The Plan for the 1967-1970 period provides for the creation of 1.5 million jobs at the enormous cost of 830-840 billion zloty, set aside for investment. Yet, according to the calculations of the demographers (Holzer's article in *Trybuna Ludu* published before the 15th Plenum of the CC of the PUWP), the increase in the working age population during that period will amount to two million. This means that if the Plan is fulfilled, there will be no jobs for about 500,000 people. At the Fourth Party Congress, no increases in real wages were promised; from published data (28% increase in individual consumption alongside an 18% increase in employment), one may conclude that, if the Plan is executed ideally, the average real wage will increase by about 10%, by about two per cent yearly, during the Five Year Plan period. However, Professor Kalecki has shown that necessary raises alone consume nearly two per cent of the wage fund every year.

Apart from this, there is a growing differential between the earning levels of workers, on the one hand, and managers, engineers and technicians, on the other. According to official data, in the 1960-1963 period, the average real income per capita in families of white-collar workers employed in industry rose by 11.6%, while the increase for workers' families was only 2.6%. In the CC's report to the Fourth Party Congress, it was mentioned that the investment fund has been so calculated as to make possible "at least a stabilization of real wages," that is, on the brink of the inflationary barrier. This means that workers' real wages in the comnig five years must be lowered somewhat if the Plan is to be realized. But in all the 20 years of the Polish Peoples' Republic, investments always cost more than planned and were never completed within the allotted time. Nothing indicates that the coming Five Year Plan period will be an exception. The sum of 840 billion zloty will probably turn out to be insufficient for carrying out a business-like program of investment and the collapse of this program will mean a drastic rise in unemployment. It will be necessary to find additional means for the realization of the investment program. Since these means can only be found by subtracting them from the consumption fund, the assumption that real wages can be stabilized will not prove correct. A substantial fall in real wages will result and the inflationary barrier will be broken.

The possibilities of supplementing the investment fund by lowering real wages are limited, however, for economic and political reasons. Therefore, it is likely that the investment program for the 1966-1970 period will not be fulfilled after all and no way will be found of creating the 1.5 million new jobs. The number of people for whom there will be no jobs will then exceed half a million.

The mass proportions of unemployment will probably compel the economic bosses to employ some of these people despite the shortage of jobs. In that case, the nominal wage fund will rise while production will not increase. This will cause a disruption in the balance of the market. Prices will soar and real wages will fall further while hundreds of thousands of people of working age will still find no work.

As can be seen, in a growing crisis the system not only deprives the working class of the prospect of an improved material situation, it is not even able to assure the maintenance of earnings at the present level or the retention of jobs.

By treating social consumption as a necessary evil, the bureaucracy tries to keep the earnings of numerous categories of hired workers at subsistence levels. This includes not only industrial, construction and transport workers, but also the large majority of white collar employees in telecommunications, the communal economy, trade, the health services, education and the lower echelons of civil service. This mass of low-paid white collar employees differs in no way from the working class in terms of their material situation and future prospects. Everything we have said about the workers' material conditions of existence when the system is in economic crisis applies to the large majority of all employees outside agriculture.

Industrialization has brought a substantial improvement in the social and cultural conditions of the working class. Education has become universal and the young have been given an opportunity to advance since university education has become accessible to all. Many of these achievements—state housing at low rents, free medical care, social benefits, etc.—constitute an indispensable part of the historically determined subsistence level, given the low level of the working wage. In crisis conditions, the bureaucracy first limits all expenditures which might be called "investments in the human being" and this hits the poorest categories of the population hardest, the working class, the low-paid white collar employees and the poorer peasantry.

Despite the very bad housing situation, Poland is one of the last on the European list in constructing housing. It has also adopted a cooperative system which is supposed to supply 60% of the apartments in the next Five Year Plan. That is why the costs of building apartment houses were transferred from the state budget to individual incomes which means that apartments will not be obtained by those who need them most, but by those who can pay for them. For a worker, whose wages are hardly sufficient to survive, it is practically impossible to get an apartment.

Cuts in cultural expenses together with higher prices in this area cause a decline in cultural activities. Theater audiences are smaller and periodical and book editions, including textbooks, drastically decreased. This particularly hurts workers' families which exist on a minimum subsistence level and for whom the higher prices of books, theater and movie tickets, etc., amounts to giving up many elementary cultural goods.

Cuts in expenses for higher education, in particular for scholarships, student cafeterias and dormitories, make it difficult for youngsters from workers', peasants' and lower middle class families to attend universities. Their percentage in higher education decreases: a money standard limits their rights to education and social advancement.

In a growing crisis, working conditions inevitably deteriorate. The growing danger of unemployment makes managers and supervisors more willful and greatly facilitates official pressure on the workers. Formerly, exploitation was covered up by compulsory, sloganized and sometimes authentic enthusiasm. The powers-that-be liked to put on overalls and prided themselves on their working class origins. They decorated shock workers and found it unfitting to pay the manager ten times as much as the worker. Today, the authorities wear elegant suits and the manager who knows best how to squeeze the surplus product out of the workers is a positive hero of socialist construction, while his villa and car are visible symbols of his social prestige and civic virtue. Today, exploitation is evident and visible to all, and its tool is not propaganda or forced enthusiasm but the whip of economic penalty, of administrative coercion and—in cases of organized attempts at resistance—of police violence. Today, the trade unions, jointly with the government and together with the managements, execute resolutions and decisions on firing workers (Operation "R").

Thus the crisis worsens the material, cultural and social situation of the working class, intensifies the degree of its captivity in its place of work and completely deprives it of prospects for the realization of its minimal interest within the framework of prevailing production and social relations. *It forces the working class to come out against the system in defense of the present level of its material and spiritual existence.*

THE BUREAUCRACY WILL NOT WILLINGLY give up to the working class even one zloty and, in conditions of economic crisis and lack of reserves, it has nothing to give up under pressure. In this situation, any large-scale strike action cannot but transform itself into a political conflict with the bureaucracy. For the working class, it is the only way to change its situation. *Today, at a time when the system is going through a general crisis, the interest of the working class lies in revolution*: the overthrow of the bureaucracy and the present relations of production, gaining control over one's own labor and its product, control over the production goals— the introduction of an economic, social and political system based on workers' democracy. The interests of the vast majority of white collar employees coincide with those of the working class.

For the countryside, the crisis means mass reductions in the number of worker-peasants, the reappearance of rural over-population and the loss of sources of income outside agriculture which support poor peasants and a large number of small farms. For the majority of peasants, it means not only a lack of prospects for improvement but an absolute worsening of their material situation and a danger of their farms failing. Only the small minority of rich peasants can benefit from this through an increased supply of cheap labor and cheap land which will open possibilities for capitalization. But even this richest group feels the fiscal pressure of the state as a limitation on its possibilities of accumulation and capitalist development. Therefore, despite the fact that the present agricultural policy is relatively the most suitable from its point of view, its attitude toward the system is hostile and it will not lend active support to the ruling bureaucracy.

If society in general is deprived of perspectives, it is the *youth* who experience this most painfully. Unemployment is a disaster for the working class as a whole but young people just reaching working age are the first to be jobless. Transition to cooperative building deprives the majority of city dwellers of the chance to improve its housing situation, but young people about to marry and start a family find it most difficult to find a place of their own. The danger of rural over-population threatens the well-being of the majority of peasants, but would be worst for members of the younger generation who would not find jobs in industry, while at the fathers' or elder brothers' farms they would, at best, have the status of agricultural laborers. Inadequate investments for higher education retard the development of the whole of society, but inflict the greatest damage on the children of workers, peasants and small town dwellers.

Since the youth are finding it particularly difficult to secure a place in the life of the community and are among the most seriously hurt by the economic, social, ideological and moral crisis, it constitutes a potentially revolutionary element in every stratum.

It would appear that today the *technocracy* is the chief pillar of bureaucratic power in society since it is bound to the ruling class by its privileges and special role in the productive process. Reality would undoubtedly conform to appearance if this technocracy could achieve its natural aspirations within the framework of the existing system. Before 1956, it was a stratum of badly paid supervisors whose salaries were much smaller than those of the small pre-war groups of administrators at the service of capital. But along with the post-war impetus to industry, a managerial cadre emerged and the directors' chairs were filled by people who owed their advancement, and everything else, to the system.

Today, the technocracy has become a stable stratum conscious of its own interests. It enjoys the privileges of high consumption and is in conflict with the working class in its daily supervisory function and in its hankering for a form of "managerial socialism." On the other hand, we have seen that the class goal of production under the present system is alien to the interests of the technocracy which acts against the goals set up by the bureaucracy whenever it has an opportunity to exercise any initiative. That is why the managerial stratum is deprived, not only of all influence on general economic decision-making, but also of the right to decide on matters of fundamental significance for its own plants and its own work. In the existing system, the technocrats can be nothing more than executors and supervisors who cannot realize their own aspirations. They yearn for decentralization of management based on the Yugoslav model, thereby seeking a change in the production relations. The slogan, "power to the experts," popular with this group, expresses both the managers' opinion of what the social range of democracy should be in their kind of socialism as well as their hostility toward the existing system and the central political bureaucracy at its head.

The interests of the technocracy, exceeding the limitations of the existing system, drive it into opposition to the ruling bureaucracy.

We have seen also that the entire working class, the majority of low-paid salaried employees, almost the entire peasantry (with the exception of the richest group), the youth—in other words, the overwhelming majority of the population—have no prospect of improving their lot within the framework of the existing system. On the contrary, the growing crisis worsens their material, social and cultural living conditions. Under these circumstances, the bureaucracy is deprived of social support and must rely on blatant economic, administrative and political coercion which clearly reveals the class nature of its dictatorship. The control of the political police over society is tightened, not because it is again to become a Moloch that will devour the Party itself but because, in all strata, hostility to the ruling bureaucracy is sharpening and any autonomous organization of social forces in this situation signifies mortal danger for the system. The legislation of total Stalinist dictatorship—the so-called "Small Criminal Code"—has been dusted off.

BY ITS VERY NATURE, the bureaucracy destroys social initiative since its rule is based on a monopoly of social organization and the atomization of independent social forces. This tendency is reinforced during times of crisis when any authentic social initiative becomes a more dangerous threat to the bureaucracy. Initiatives connected with the development of social thinking and with the enrichment of cultural and ideological life—discussion clubs, cultural societies, etc.—are subjected to strict control and treated by the authorities as a potential danger. The same applies to all signs of independent ideological-political activity and to discussions in the livelier youth and Party organizations, something that the members of the Party and SYU at the university know from their own experience.

Since it no longer has the possibility of imposing its hegemony on the rest of society, the bureaucracy has no ideology of its own; nothing has replaced the official Stalinist doctrine which was shattered in 1956–1957. The bureaucracy justifies its political and economic moves in the name of the "national interest." The national interest, if it is not the interest of the various classes and strata in society, can only be the interest of the class in whose hands state power resides. No matter how hard the bureaucracy tries to obscure its class interest by presenting it as the general national interest, nationalism preached from a position of power in a period of social crisis, has little chance of gaining social support.

Having no official, coherent ideological system, while at the same time controlling the sum total of collective life and all forms of ideological life in the country by means of organizational, administrative and police methods, the bureaucracy seeks to eliminate all signs of ideological independence in a time of general crisis. For ideology is the consciousness of people acting socially in conditions of crisis. When the interests of the overwhelming majority of society can no longer be satisfied within the framework of the system and when they turn against it, then authentic ideology and social activity reflecting the interests of given strata must, ultimately, turn against the bureaucracy.

This situation has especially sharp repercussions on the creative intelligentsia, for its social function is the scientific formulation of social thought and the artistic expression of ideas. The ideological crisis in society signifies a crisis in creativity for this stratum and all attempts to overcome it and achieve ideological independence for its creative members are administratively repressed. Engaged scholars, writers and artists are discriminated against by publishing houses and cultural policy makers. They are denied access to mass media, i.e., the chance to practice their profession; socio-literary periodicals which exhibit even a minimum degree of independence are replaced by publications which are then boycotted by the most eminent creative people; the intensification of censorship narrows down still further the already small margin of professional freedom among the creative intelligentsia. In this way, the ideological crisis becomes the source of a crisis in cultural creativity.

The ideological crisis also brings in its wake a crisis of moral values and norms, especially for youth in the process of forming their views and ideals. What results is cynicism, crude careerism, hooliganism; mass thefts, too, are not just an economic phenomenon.

As the economic crisis cannot be overcome within the framework of present production relations, so, too, the general social crisis cannot be overcome within the limits imposed by prevailing social relations. A solution is possible only through the overthrow of prevailing production and social relations. *Revolution is a necessity for development.*

No social class sides with the bureaucracy in crisis. At best, the rich peasants and petty bourgeoisie might remain neutral. But only the working class, because of its conditions of life and work, *is compelled* to overthrow the bureaucracy. The essential origins of the economic and social crisis lie, as we have seen, in the production relations that prevail in the sector of heavy industry; that is, in the relations into which the working class and the central political bureaucracy enter mutually in the productive process. Revolution is thus, first of all, the conflict between these two fundamental classes in an industrialized society. That is why the working class must be the chief and leading force of revolution. The revolution that will overthrow the bureaucratic system will be a proletarian revolution.

It is often said that a tremendous power apparatus, having at its disposal modern means of material coercion, is sufficient for the ruling class to perpetuate its power even without any social backing. Despite appearances of modernity in the argument, this is an error as old as class society and the state itself. In October 1956, we saw that a powerful coercive machine in Hungary proved helpless and collapsed within a few days. The working class produces and transports weapons, serves in the armed forces, produces the entire material potential of the state. The walls of prisons, barracks and arsenals are durable, not because they have been built of solid materials, but because they are guarded by the authority of the powers-that-be, by fear and accommodation to the prevailing social order. These psychological walls allow the ruling powers to secure its position atop the walls of brick. But a deepening social crisis undermines the psychological walls that are the real defense of the ruling power and as a revolutionary situation matures, the walls of brick, too, will crumble. In view of the impossibility of overcoming the crisis within the framework of the bureaucratic system, *revolution is inevitable.*

9.
THE INTERNATIONAL PROBLEMS OF THE REVOLUTION

WE ARE TOLD: "We live in the center of European conflicts. The world is divided into camps, and both sides have atomic weapons. All revolutionary movements in this situation are crimes against the nation and against humanity. The Polish 'raison d'etat,' following from the international situation and our geographical situation, demands our silence and obedience. Otherwise, we are menaced with atomic annihilation or, at best, with intervention by the tanks of a friendly power, as happened in Hungary. Under such conditions, to analyze social structures, to discuss surplus value, to work out political programs—these are occupations which are either irrational or simply harmful. In order to build socialism one must first of all *exist.*"

Since this is a political argument, it is not a matter of indifference who says it and why. It is said first of all by the very representatives of the ruling state power although they do not always dot all the "i's." It is also said by people who reluctantly admit to connections with the government, but willingly suggest that, at the bottom of their souls, they are opposition-minded. They, nevertheless, proclaim obedience to the ruling state power, as they defend it. As propagandists of the system they speak; as alleged members of the opposition they are silent; their resistance does not go beyond the intimate area of their spiritual experience. In point of fact, therefore, they belong in the camp of the ruling state power and they plead the cause of the ruling bureaucracy.

This argumentation is, to put it delicately, somewhat equivocal: the leaders and propagandists of a system which has at its disposal all means of coercion and destruction, call on the masses for obedience in the name of maintaining peace. As a typical argument "from a position of strength," this blackmail can be rational and convincing. Let us therefore calmly consider this reasoning without deluding ourselves that it is a form of gentle persuasion.

1) This thinking is based on the assumption that revolution is the result of a criminal conspiracy against internal or world peace. It is the traditional argument of all anti-revolutionary ideologies and well known in the history of the workers' movement. It is typical police thinking. In reality, revolutions are the result of economic and social crises.

From the social point of view, revolution is always an act of force which pits the strength of a social movement against that of the ruling power. But revolution is the act of an enormous majority of society directed against the rule of a minority that is in political crisis and whose apparatus of coercion has been weakened. That is why revolution does not necessarily have to be carried out by force of arms. The possibility of avoiding civil war depends on such factors as the level of consciousness and organization of the revolutionary movement which limit the degree of chaos and the possibilities of armed counteraction.

The real crime against the internal peace of the country is committed by the ruling bureaucracy, which first tries to disorganize the masses, deprive them of political consciousness and then uses armed force to try to break their revolutionary movement. We remember Poznan and Budapest.

2) The argument of Soviet tanks. It is said that an eventual revolution in Poland would inevitably lead to Soviet armed intervention, the result of which, from the military point of view, is not open to doubt. Those who advance this view assume that everything takes place in "one country in isolation" which, by way of exception, is torn by class struggles while in neighboring countries there are no classes but only regular armies with a given number of planes and tanks. For them, the revolution neither crosses national boundaries nor has an effect beyond them.

This typical "political realism" completely contradicts historical experience. Revolutionary crises have always been of an international nature. 1956 was no exception, but the bureaucracy then had at its disposal economic and social reserves which enabled it to handle the crisis by a reform maneuver. This made it possible to put a brake on the development of the revolution in Poland, to prevent a revolutionary situation from arising in Czechoslovakia, the GDR and the USSR and, thereby, permitted the Hungaian revolution to be isolated and crushed. The present phase of the crisis is marked by a lack of the necessary reserves for such a maneuver. This is true not only in Poland but also in Czechoslovakia, the GDR and Hungary and even of the USSR itself. It is difficult to foresee in which of these countries the revolution will begin; it is certain, however, that it will not end where it begins. The crisis in these countries cannot be mitigated, even temporarily, by reforms and concessions because there is nothing more to concede or to reform within the framework of the system. Under these conditions, the revolutionary movement must spread to the whole camp, while the possibilities of armed intervention on the part of the Soviet bureaucracy (if it is still in power) will not be measured by the number of its tanks and planes but by the degree of tension of class conflicts within the USSR.

The anti-bureaucratic revolution undoubtedly undermines the political stabilization of neo-capitalism though it obviously more directly menaces the central political bureaucracy. In any case, it is improbable that Western imperialism, which would gladly take the place of the overthrown bureaucracy, would resort to intervention for that purpose. The working class in the developed Western countries has won a relatively wide margin of democratic freedoms for itself and for society. Therefore, war requires proper preparation of public opinion. Understanding this, an armed crusade against the countries of the anti-bureaucratic revolution is most implausible since it would run counter to public opinion, lead to mass resistance and an active anti-war struggle by the working class which, over there, is a well organized and powerful political force. Moreover, neo-capitalism is threatened by the colonial revolution. A final deterrent to imperialist intervention against an anti-bureaucratic revolution is that it would threaten to escalate into a suicidal, world-wide nuclear conflict.

3) The atom bomb is a modern addition to the traditional arsenal of anti-revolutionary arguments. Today, when the stocks of nuclear weapons are more than enough to destroy the world, the governing elites of the two great blocs which share power in the world decry revolution as a crime against internal peace and all humanity. Those who possess the arsenals filled with the means of nuclear annihilation, the leading circles of imperialism and the international [central political] bureaucracy demand obedience from the masses in the name of avoiding a world-wide nuclear war.

A world nuclear conflict would be absurd from the point of view of the goals of both great blocs; it would lead to the destruction, if not of the whole of mankind, at least of the major powers and of the parts of the world that are most thickly populated and economically and culturally advanced. It would be suicide. The two great blocs don't want mutual destruction in any case, but are engaged in an economic, political and diplomatic competition based on a division into spheres of influence. In their struggle against the revolutionary movement, atomic weapons are a means of blackmail. It is a well-known fact, however, that since the end of World War II, revolutionary wars are continually being waged in various parts of the world, while at the same time, and *independent of them,* the two great blocs, having atomic weapons at their disposal, carry on their politics of tension and rapprochment. This was pointed out recently by the leaders of the Chinese bureaucracy when their conflict with the Soviet bureaucracy and their attempt to strengthen their independence and international position drove them to an alliance with the forces of the colonial revolution.

The bureaucracy speaks a great deal about the need to maintain peace on the basis of the status quo. But every time its rule was threatened, it did not hesitate to use armed might. It used tanks against the demonstrating Berlin workers in June 1953; it did the same against the Poznan workers in 1956 and against the workers of Novocherkassk in 1962; it launched a regular war against the working class in Hungary.

The leaders of the imperialist countries compete with the bureaucracy in peace phraseology. But the history of the last 20 years is filled with armed interventions and wars against the colonial revolution: from the crushing of the liberation struggle of the Greek partisans, through Korea, Vietnam, Algeria, Cuba and right up to the Congo and the latest acts of aggression against the Democratic Republic of Vietnam.

4) It is understandable that the ideological spokesmen of the ruling classes do not like to reflect about the social causes of the war danger, while they hold as undesirable, "surplus value considerations." In reality, this matter has never been as urgent as it is today, when the alienation of labor assumes material forms which threaten the existence of mankind, when the surplus product created by the workers of the West, by the nations exploited by imperialism, and by the workers of the USSR is turned against them in the classical form of police, prisons, marines, tanks, to which is now added the means of atomic annihilation.

The sources of the war danger are the growing social conflicts which give birth to and deepen the crisis in the world rule of the system of anti-popular dictatorship. This is true in the first place of imperialism which, being unable to maintain its rule over the backward countries, wages wars of intervention and continually embarks on new political adventures of "brinksmanship." But this is also true of the international bureaucracy; we remember the Berlin crisis of 1961, the provocative installation of Soviet rocket launching sites in Cuba and the threat to the Cuban revolution and world peace which followed; we remember the operations undertaken by Soviet tanks in Berlin and the war of intervention launched against the Hungarian revolution.

Every assault on revolutionary movements strengthens anti-popular dictatorships and increases the risk of war. The danger of war can be done away with finally only by eliminating its social sources—imperialism and bureaucratic dictatorship. The possibilities for limiting this danger today and of its complete elimination in the future are afforded mankind by an organized international revolutionary movement conscious of its goals.

5) Bureaucracy and the revolutionary movement in the world. The young Soviet republic was able to defend itself successfully against the intervention of the imperialist countries thanks to the struggle of the working class in the West and the wave of revolutionary movements which shook the world toward the end of World War I and after the victory of the Russian revolution. The maintenance and general development of Soviet Russia as *a workers' state* depended on the results of the revolutionary struggles in other countries, especially in the industrialized

countries of the West. Lenin, Trotsky and the other Bolshevik leaders realized that only another revolutionary power could be a genuine ally of the proletarian dictatorship. That is why the ideology and foreign policy of Soviet Russia in that early period had an internationalist character. As the Soviet state became bureaucratized and the ruling elite was transformed into a ruling class, an international revolutionary movement could not serve as a natural ally of the Soviet bureaucratic class. The movement had to be—and was—subordinated to the directives of the Soviet bureaucracy to provide a convenient bargaining counter and tool for the realization of the state interests of the USSR's ruling bureaucracy. We know the results.

On the other hand, every independent and victorious revolution is a menace to the bureaucracy. For revolution is a sovereign act by the masses whose example and contagious ideas strike at the ideological hegemony of the bureaucracy over its own subjects. Moreover, victorious revolutions do not subordinate themselves to the dictates of the Soviet bureaucracy; hence they threaten the rule of the international monolith, which is also dangerous for the internal monolith. The first country where an independent, victorious revolution took place after World War II was Yugoslavia, the second China. We know the results.

That is why the Soviet bureaucracy follows the principle: "socialism" will reach as far as its army. In the name of this principle, it first tried to subordinate to its own police and its own bureaucrats the Spanish revolution, which it then betrayed; it forbade the French and Italian Communists to carry on a struggle for power in the 1945-1946 revolutionary situation; it betrayed the Greek revolution; it tried to pressure the Chinese Communists to abandon the struggle against Chiang Kai-shek's army.

Snatching countries from capitalist domination had been, and is, a factor that favors the revolutionary struggle against imperialism. But the bureaucratization of those countries is a factor which puts a brake on the development of the colonial revolution and on the struggle of the working class of the highly developed capitalist countries. Through its foreign policy based on the sharing of spheres of influence with imperialism and on maintaining the status quo, through its ideology which sanctions this policy and finally through its influence on the official Communist Parties, the international bureaucracy opposes the anti-capitalist revolution. The colonial revolution, however, escapes its control; it is successfully organized and directed by groups which stand outside the official Communist Parties. Witness Cuba, witness Algeria.

The control exerted by the international bureaucracy over the world Communist movement is going through a crisis that has been deepened profoundly by the first anti-bureaucratic revolutions in Poland and Hungary. A victorious anti-bureaucratic revolution will put an end to the dictatorship's control and prove to be the natural ally of the world revolutionary movement.

10.
PROGRAMME

THUS FAR WE HAVE considered the revolution as the gravedigger of the old order. It also creates a new society. Is the working class, which must be the main and leading force of the revolution, capable of developing a real, viable program?

The class interest of the workers demands the abolition of the bureaucratic ownership of the means of production and of exploitation. This does not mean that the worker is to receive, in the form of a working wage, the full equivalent of the product of his labor. The level of development of the productive forces in a modern society necessitates a division of labor in which there are unproductive sectors, supported by the material product created by the worker. Therefore, under conditions of a workers' democracy, it will also be necessary to set aside from the total product a part earmarked for accumulation, for the maintenance and development of health services, education, science, culture, social benefits and those expenditures for administration and for the apparatus of political power which the working class will recognize as indispensable. The essence of exploitation is not that the working wage represents only a part of the value of the newly created product but that the surplus product is taken away from the worker by force and that the process of capital accumulation is alien to his interests, while the unproductive sectors serve to maintain and strengthen the rule of a bureaucracy (or bourgeoisie) over production and over society, and thus in the first place, over the labor and social life of the working class.

To abolish exploitation means, therefore, to create a system in which the organized working class will be master of its own labor and the resulting product; in which it will set the goals of social production, decide on the sharing and use of the national income, hence define the size and purpose of investments, the size and disbursement of expenditures for social benefits, health services, education, science and culture, the amount for the power apparatus and its current tasks. In brief, a system in which the working class will exercise economic, social and political power in the state.

How should the working class and its state be organized in order that it might rule over its own labor and its product?

1) If there is no workers' democracy in the factory, there can be none in the state on any long-term basis. For it is only in the factory that the worker is a worker, that he fulfills his fundamental social function. If he were to remain a slave in his place of work, then any freedom outside the place of work would soon become "Sunday freedom," fictitious freedom.

The working class cannot rule over its own labor and its product without controlling the conditions and goals of its toil in the factory. To that end, it must organize itself in the plants into Workers' Councils in order to run the factories. The manager must be made into a functionary subordinate to the Council, controlled, hired or dismissed by the Council.

However, these days, all key decisions relating to the management of an enterprise are made centrally. Under these conditions, the Workers' Council would, in practice, be deprived of power. The manager is closely bound up with the offices which make the decisions—the central apparatus of economic management. In this situation, the Workers' Council would inevitably be reduced to an adjunct to the management, as is the case with the present-day Conferences of Workers' Self-Government.

To manage enterprises through its Workers' Councils, the working class must make the enterprises independent, creating the preliminary conditions for workers' democracy and, at the same time, adapting management relationships to the new class goal of production (as we have already shown, the system of centralized management is an organizational tool of production for the sake of production, whereas production for the sake of consumption requires a decentralized system). Thus, while taking the first step toward realizing its program, the working class achieves that which is most far-reaching and progressive in the program of technocracy: the independence of enterprises. But the working class and the technocracy each imbue this concept with a fundamentally different social content. To the technocracy, independence of an enterprise means that management has full powers in the factory. For the working class, it means self-government for the working force. That is why the working class must go beyond plant management by the Councils. Workers' self-rule, limited to the level of the enterprise, would inevitably become fictitious and a cover for the power of management in the factory and for the rule of a new technocratic bureaucracy; exploitation would be maintained and the former state of chaos would return in a new form.

Basic decisions relating to the sharing and use of the national income naturally have a general social character; that is, they are made on an economy-wide scale and, therefore, they can only be made centrally. If these central decisions were to remain outside the influence of the working class, it would not rule over the product that it has created and over its own labor.

2) That is why in addition to factory councils, the working class will have to organize itself into a nationwide system of Councils of Workers' Delegates, headed by a Central Council of Delegates. Through the system of councils, the working class will determine the national economic plant and maintain permanent control over its execution. As a result, the Councils at all levels will become organs of economic, political, legislative and executive power. They will be truly elective offices, since the electors, organized according to the natural principle of production, will be able at any time to recall their representatives and appoint new ones in their place. In this way, the representatives of working forces in the factories will become the backbone of proletarian state power.

3) If, however, the workers' representatives in the Central Council of Delegates were to have only one draft plan for the division of the national income laid before them by the government or by the leadership of the sole political party, their role would be limited to a mechanical act of voting. As we noted earlier, a monopolistic ruling party cannot be a workers' party; it inevitably becomes the party of the dictatorship over the working class, an organization of a bureaucracy designed to keep the workers and the whole of society disorganized and in line.

For the council system to become the expression of the organized will, organized opinion and organized activity of the masses, *the working class must organize itself along multi-party lines.* In practice, a workers' multi-party system means the right of every political group which has its base in the working class to publish its own paper, to propagate its own program through mass media, to organize cadres of activists and agitators, i.e., to form a party. A workers' multi-party system requires freedom of speech, press and association, *the abolition of preventive censorship,* full freedom of scholarly research, of literary and artistic creativity. Without the freedom to elaborate, publish, express various ideological trends, without full freedom for the creative intelligentsia, there is no workers' democracy.

In the workers' multi-party system, various parties will propose plans for the division of the national income to the Central Council of Delegates, creating conditions for discerning alternatives and for freedom of choice for the Central representatives of the working class and for factory workers electing and recalling their delegates.

We speak of a workers' multi-party system, although it would serve no purpose or even be possible, to limit membership in the parties to workers only. The working class character of the multi-party system would follow from the nature of the state power, organized as a system of councils. This means that parties seeking to influence the center of political power would be obliged to win influence among the workers.

By the same token, we are against the parliamentary system. The experience of both 20-year periods shows that it carried no guarantee against dictatorship and, even in its most perfect form, it is not a form of people's power. In the parliamentary system, parties compete for votes. Once the votes have been cast, election programs can be tossed into the wastebasket. The deputies in parliament feel close only to the leadership of the party which nominated them. The electorate, artificially arranged in purely formal districts is atomized and the right to recall a deputy is fictitious. The citizen's participation in political life is reduced to reading statements by political leaders, listening to them on radio or watching them on television, while once every four or five years, he goes to the ballot box to decide which party's representatives are to rule him. Everything happens with his mandate, but without his participation. In addition, parliament is a purely legislative body, which permits executive power to emerge as the only real authority, dominated by men of economic power. Thus, in the parliamentary system, the working class and the whole of society, on the strength of their own vote, are deprived of influence on the center of power.

As against this formal, periodic voting, we propose the regular participation of the working class, through its Councils, parties and trade unions, in economic and political decision-making at all levels. In capitalist society, above parliament, stands the bourgeoisie, disposing of the surplus product; in the bureaucratic system, above the fiction of parliament, the central political bureaucracy rules indivisibly. In a system of workers' democracy, if it takes a parliamentary form, the working class will stand above it, organized into councils and having at its disposal the material basis of society's existence—the product of its labor.

4) The working class cannot decide directly, but only through its political representation at the central level, how to divide the product it has created. But as its interests are not entirely uniform, contradictions between the decisions of workers' representatives and the aspirations of particular sections of the working class are unavoidable. The very fact of separating the function of management from the function of production carries with it the possibility of alienation of the elected power, at the level of both the enterprise and the state. If the workers were deprived of the possibility of self-defense in the face of the decisions of the representative system, apart from their right to vote (i.e. apart from that very system), then it would turn against those whom it is supposed to represent. If the working class was deprived of the possibilities of self-defense in its own state, workers' democracy would be fraudulent. This defense should be assured by *trade unions completely independent of the state and with the right to organize economic and political strikes.* The various parties, competing for influence in the trade unions, would struggle for the preservation of their working class character.

5) To prevent the institutions of workers' democracy from being reduced to a facade, behind which the old disorder would make a comeback, their democratic forms must be the living expression of the activity of the working masses. Administrators, experts and politicians have the necessary time and knowledge to bother with public affairs while the worker is obliged to stand next to his machine. To take an active part in public life, the worker, too, must be provided with the necessary time and knowledge. This requires a certain number of hours to be set aside weekly from the required paid working time to insure *the universal education of the workers.* During those hours, workers grouped into production complexes will discuss draft economic plans submitted by different parties for the country, factory or region which are too difficult for popular presentation only if an attempt is made to conceal their class content. The representatives of political parties participating in these hours of workers' education will bring both their programs and the working class closer to each other.

6) In a workers' democracy it will be impossible to preserve the political police or the regular army in any form. The anti-democratic character of the political police is obvious to everyone; on the other hand, the ruling classes have had more success in spreading myths about the regular army.

The regular army tears hundreds of thousands of young people away from their environment. They are isolated in barracks, brainwashed of independent thinking through brutal methods, and taught, instead, a mechanical performance of every order issued by their professional commanders, locked in a rigid hierarchy. This organization of armed force is separated from society in order that it may, more easily, be directed against society. The regular army, like the political police, is by its very nature a tool of anti-democratic dictatorship. As long as it is maintained, a clique of Generals may always prove stronger than all the parties and councils.

It is said that the regular army is necessary to defend the state. This is true in the case of an anti-democratic dictatorship, where, other than by terror, it is impossible to force the large mass of people to defend a state that does not belong to them. On the other hand, if the masses were allowed to carry arms outside the military organization, it would create a mortal danger for the system. Consequently, a regular army, for such a system, is the only possible form of defense force.

We have already seen, during the revolutionary wars in Vietnam, Algeria and Cuba, that the armed workers and peasants—if they know what they are fighting for and if they identify their interests with those of the revolution—are not worse soldiers than those in the regular army. This is especially true for small countries threatened by the counter-revolutionary intervention of a foreign power. It has no chance with a regular army; it can defend itself successfully by a people's war. Regular armies are necessary to aggressors who undertake colonial wars and wars of intervention; they are necessary to the anti-democratic dictatorships in order to keep the masses obedient. This is evident especially in Latin American countries where the army has exclusively the internal function of the police. It can also be observed elsewhere—in Poland, too—as we saw during the events in Poznan. Whether or not the army and the workers actually clash, the regular army always remains an instrument of tyranny over the working class and society, just as a club always remains a means of beating, whether or not its owner actually puts it to that use. In a system of workers' democracy, the regular army does not insure defense against the counter-revolution; on the contrary, it may become the source and the tool of the counter-revolutionary camp. It must therefore be abolished.

To make democracy indestructible, the working class should be armed. This applies, first of all, to the workers in larger industries who should be organized into a workers' militia under the aegis of the Workers' Councils. The military experts who will train the workers' militia will be employed by the Workers' Councils and remain subordinated to them. In this way, the basic military repressive force in the state will be directly tied to the working class which will always be ready to defend its own state and its own revolution.

For technical reasons, it is unavoidable to maintain permanent military units within specialized divisions such as the navy, airforce, rocketry, etc. The soldiers for those divisions should be recruited among the workers of heavy industry, and during their military service they should remain in touch with their factory teams and retain all their workers' rights.

8) Agricultural production plays an essential part in the economy, and the peasantry too important a role in society for the workers' program to bypass the affairs of the countryside. The future of agriculture lies, without doubt, with large, specialized industrialized and nationalized enterprises. The technical base for such an organization of agricultural production can only be created by the industrialization of agriculture. This requires enormous investments, whose realization is a problem for the distant future. Under present technical-economic conditions, all attempts at collectivization mean depriving the peasant of the land he owns which can be achieved only against his will through the methods of police dictatorship. The result would be a fall in production and a police dictatorship victimizing the working class itself. Such collectivization can be reconciled only with a bureaucratic system; it spells death for workers' democracy.

The free, unlimited interplay of market forces, under conditions of individual ownership of land, and given the present structure of agriculture, leads to capitalist-type farming. It deprives owners of small and scattered holdings of the possibility of concentrating their means of investment, necessary for their development, and consequently shifts the major part of the means of investment in the countryside to the richest farms. It means the rationalization of the rural economy through a deep crisis, bankrupting the poorest holdings; and it means unemployment and high prices for necessities for the industrial working class. This is acceptable to the technocracy which is naturally sympathetic to capitalist farming, but unacceptable to a workers' democracy.

For the working class, the goal of production is the development of the consumption of the broad mass of people who today live at subsistence level. As we have already seen, the bureaucracy pushes the consumption of the majority of villages even below that level, deprives the peasant economy of its surpluses and agriculture of any prospects of development, because it seeks to minimize the real expenditure on labor and regards social consumption as a necessary evil.

The interests of the working class lie in overthrowing these relationships between the peasant economy and the state; it demands a rapid development of agricultural production—the basis for increased consumption—through the development of the mass of small and medium individual holdings. This makes the working class the spokesman for the majority of peasants and creates the basis for a real alliance between them. To realize their common interests it is necessary, first of all, to overcome the "price scissors" which deprives small and medium peasant holdings of the material base for development, and to tax progressively the richest farms. Second, that part of the product of the peasant's labor intercepted by the state in the form of taxes or in any other way must be—after subtracting sums corresponding to the peasants' contribution to administrative expenditures—returned to the countryside in the form of social and cultural investments and as state economic and technical aid to assist small and dwarf holdings.

To ACHIEVE THIS, the peasantry needs to organize itself on an economic basis and elect its own political representatives. It must set up its own production organizations and find new perspectives for the almost 60% of the peasantry which vegetates on small holdings and has labor surpluses; it is inadmissable to allow investments in industry to be blown up out of all proportion. This requires the proper use of labor surpluses in intensive additional production, such as livestock breeding, vegetable and fruit cultivation and such industries as meat packing and fruit canning. This is very difficult, and in the case of processing plants, impossible to achieve with the scattered forces of smallholdings. The precondition for success is the creation of associations of small and medium holdings, having at their disposal a labor surplus. These associations, based on the land they possess, on cooperation and on state aid in the form of low-interest credits, participation in small investments, transport guarantees, etc., will then set up small processing plants and, also in common, organize their supplies and marketing. This is the cheapest way to increase the production of deficit-bearing agricultural produce and to invigorate the underdeveloped food industry. It is also the only way of intensifying the work of dwarf and small holdings and simultaneously employing on the spot, the existing labor surplus.

Peasant holdings must be provided with conditions favoring specialization of production, without which there can be no rational husbandry. At the same time, in their contacts with state purchasing enterprises, peasant producers must be organized to defend themselves against artificial lowering of prices. For the isolated peasant producer who enters into a "voluntary" accord with the state is helpless when faced with the state's monopoly of the market. Accordingly, apart from creating production organizations, the rural population must form its own universal *supply and marketing organization* for the peasant holdings. The richest farms, which are relatively few in number but play an important role given their size and economic strength, will then have no chance to transform themselves into capitalist enterprises; they will be short of cheap labor and cheap land that would otherwise be provided by the failure of weak holdings. The richest farms, however, will have the chance to increase their production on the basis of their own means of investment provided they are able to solve the manual labor shortage through the use of machines.

Inasmuch as industry plays the decisive role in the economy, the direction of industrial production will determine the general direction of the national economy. And the working class, which will have control of its own product will thereby create a general framework for the functions of the other sectors, including agriculture. But within these most general limits, determined by the level, structure and development of industrial production, the peasants must also control the product of their labor. The plans for development, for investments, for economic aid should not be imposed by the state on the peasant population. Otherwise, a specific apparatus of control would come into being and would, finally, also obtain control over the working class. *That is why political self-government by the peasants* is a must for the good of workers' democracy. It is made possible because the interests of the workers and peasants converge.

Economic organizations of peasant producers are not enough to give peasants control over that part of their product taken over by the state and which is to be restored to the countryside in the form of direct state investments and state aid to peasant holdings. This can be assured only by the *political representation of peasant producers on a national scale,* elected on the basis of economic organizations and peasant political parties.

8) WE DO NOT CONSIDER the anti-bureaucratic revolution to be a purely Polish affair. The economic and social contradictions we have analyzed appear in mature form in all the industrialized bureaucratic countries: in Czechoslovakia, the GDR, Hungary and the USSR. Nor do we view the revolution as the exclusive affair of the working class in bureaucratic dictatorships. The bureaucratic system, passed off as socialism by official progaganda in both East and West, compromises socialism in the eyes of the masses of developed capitalist countries. The international bureaucracy and its leading force—the Soviet bureaucracy—

fear all authentic revolutionary movements in any part of the world. Seeking internal and international stabilization of its own system, based on the division of the world into spheres of influence with capitalism, the bureaucracy suppresses revolutionary movements at home and uses its influence over foreign official Communist parties to impede the development of revolutionary movements in Latin America, Asia and Africa. The anti-bureaucratic revolution is, therefore, the concern of the international workers' movement and of the movement for colonial revolution.

Like every revolution, the anti-bureaucratic revolution threatens the established world order and, in turn, is threatened by the forces guarding that order. The international bureaucracy will try to crush the first country or countries of the victorious revolution in proportion to the internal forces it will still have at the moment of crisis. Western imperialism will try to take advantage of our revolution to supplant the dictatorship of the bureaucracy with the dictatorship of the capitalist monopolies, which is in no way better.

Our ally against the intervention of Soviet tanks is the Russian, Ukrainian, Hungarian and Czech working class. Our ally against the pressures and threats of imperialism is the working class of the industrialized West and the developing colonial revolution in the backward countries. Against an eventual accord between the international bureaucracy and the international imperialist bourgeoisie, which maintain systems of anti-popular dictatorship in their spheres of influence, we utter the traditional working class slogan: "proletarians of all countries, unite!"

THE WORKING CLASS MUST CARRY OUT all these changes in the area of political, social and economic relations in order to realize its own class interest, which is the command over its own labor and its product. Is this program realistic?

With the initial step toward its realization—making the enterprise independent—the working class would create the conditions for adapting production to needs, eliminating all waste of the economic surplus and the proper use of the intensive factors of economic growth. The same would be carried out by the technocracy, the difference being that the production goal of the working class is consumption by many, not the luxury consumption of privileged strata. That is why workers' control of production would assure the most radical resolution of the contradiction between an expanded productive potential and the low level of social consumption which impedes economic growth today.

The workers separate class interest coincides with the economic interests of the mass of low-paid white collar employees and of the small and medium holders in the countryside. In their combined numbers, they are the overwhelming majority of the rural and urban population. Since the slavery of the working class is the essential source of the slavery of other classes and strata, by emancipating itself, the working class also liberates the whole of society.

To liberate itself, it must abolish the political police; by doing this it frees the whole of society from fear and dictatorship;

It must abolish the regular army and liberate the soldier in the barracks from nightmarish oppression;

It must introduce a multi-party system, providing political freedom to the whole of society;

It must abolish preventive censorship, introduce full freedoms of the press, of scholarly and cultural creativity, of formulating and propagating various trends of social thinking. It will thereby liberate the writer, artist, scholar and journalist; it will create, on the widest possible scale, conditions for the free fulfillment by the intelligentsia of its proper social function;

It must subject the administrative apparatus to the permanent control and supervision of democratic organizations, changing existing relationships within that apparatus. Today's common civil servant will become a man free of humiliating dependence on a bureaucratic hierarchy;

It must assure the peasant control over his product, as well as economic, social and political self-government. It will thereby change the peasant from the eternal, helpless object of all power into an active citizen sharing in making decisions which shape his life and work.

Because the worker occupies the lowest position in the productive process, the working class more than any other social group, needs democracy: every incursion on democracy is first a blow against the worker. That is why workers' democracy will have the widest social base and will create the fullest conditions for the free development of the whole of society.

Because the workers' class interest most closely corresponds to the requirements for economic development and to the interests of society, the working class program is a realistic one.

Will that program be realized? That depends on the degree of ideological and organizational preparation of the working class in a revolutionary crisis and therefore also depends on the present activities of those who identify with workers' democracy.

11.
COUNTER ARGUMENTS

IN THE LAST SECTION OF OUR TEXT, we mentioned those contemporary socio-political tendencies against which the working class must conduct a political struggle: the technocracy ("managerial socialism"), the farmer's group ("the good husbandmen's socialism"); and the petty bourgeoisie ("Christian democracy").

In connection with our program and in particular with the above mentioned section, some basic criticisms have been advanced and we shall try to reply here. First, on relations with the technocracy.

"Managerial socialism" does not change the worker's position in the process of production. It maintains exploitation and is nothing but another form of dictatorship over the workers, over the majority of peasants and over the intelligentsia. We are not against it just for tactical reasons, but because we have consciously chosen the other side of the barricades. We have been accused of aiming at proletarian revolution, whereas the technocratic program would also solve the crisis but could be realized by a combination of pressure from below and reforms from above—without revolution and its attendant dangers.

We believe, first of all, that those who subscribe to this view have also chosen their side of the barricades so that we argue from opposing positions. Also, it is they who are the utopians although they use so-called realistic arguments. The technocratic system in Yugoslavia did not replace a fully formed bureaucratic system, but rose directly from the fluid post-revolutionary period in a specific international situation under specific economic conditions. It would seem that there existed in Poland in 1956-57 all the reasons and conditions necessary for the introduction of technocratic reforms: this would theoretically have solved the crisis and brought permanent stabilization. However, the bureaucracy did not allow this to happen for two reasons. First of all, it was by then a fully formed ruling class and defended by all means available to it the existing conditions of production upon which its rule is based. We have seen though that technocratic reform would mean a change in production relations. If yesterday's Marxists consider this argument anachronistic, we can point out another, equally important. Technocratic reform would give rise to a conflict of social forces, a political struggle at the highest level, an acute political crisis and broader, if transient, political freedom. It would also give autonomy to the enterprise and then the workers' teams would not have to combat the anonymous power of the State, but their own management. During the tensions that existed in 1956, this could most likely have brought further progress in the revolution and the collapse of bureaucratic rule. That the bureaucracy did not opt for technocratic reforms 8 years ago when the system still possessed economic reserves, and the new leadership undoubted authority, makes it most unlikely that the bureaucracy can effectuate such reforms today when it lacks both economic reserves and support in society. These are facts which not only a Marxist but an ordinary realist must take into account.

"Managerial socialism" can triumph, not instead of the revolution, but because of it, or after it. It may become a sort of Thermidor for workers' democracy. We do not see why we should work for such a solution. On the contrary, in our section on program, we tried to find ways to struggle against it.

We are also accused of not knowing what we are doing in pressing toward revolution. This, they say, can only lead to the victory of anti-socialist forces (like the multi-party system, abolition of political police, etc.) because either the working class is in its mass reactionary or the bourgeois forces are so powerful.

Those who follow this reasoning have also chosen their side of the barricades. They want to defend the existing system which they consider socialist against the working class (which is supposedly anti-socialist). In this line of reasoning, the bureaucracy has been identified with socialism and the defense of its rule over the masses is represented as the defense of socialism.

We believe that the reality is just the opposite—something we have tried to demonstrate in these pages. The ruling bureaucracy is anti-working class, an enemy. It represents the most powerful reactionary force since it has both state power and power over production. The elements of the traditional Right have no economic base in any decisive sector: industry, transport, construction, etc. The petty burgeoisie, so-called "private initiative" elements in the cities and the so-called "kulaks" in the countryside represent only a narrow margin of the national economy and the social structure. Of considerable importance, however, are rightist groups and currents, with the Church hierarchy in the lead, which are attached to the old reactionary symbols.

The bureaucratic system provokes natural antagonism and hate among the masses; it identifies itself with socialism but ruthlessly suppresses all opposition from the Left, thus creating conditions favorable for spreading rightist ideologies. among the masses. People look for ideological symbols to express their protest against the existing dictatorship and in the absence of opposition from the Left expressing their real interests, they find the old symbols of the traditional Right. In this manner, the bureaucratic dictatorship aids the traditional Right and even enters into agreements based on collaboration with them as with PAX and agreements with the Church hierarchy.

The only effective way of fighting the traditional Right is not the defense of the bureaucratic dictatorship but an insistent struggle against it, unmasking it from the Left. A working class program does not use nebulous symbols, but social realities. In its criticism and its radicalism, this program differentiates itself from all nationalist and clerical slogans. It turns against the very essence of the bureaucratic dictatorship and corresponds to the interests of the masses. Therefore, it has all chances of winning the support of the masses. The struggle against the governing Right and the Right in retirement is indivisible. To those who believe that workers' democracy, by introducing a multi-party system and abolishing the political police will give the rightist forces access to power, we reply: We are not talking of a supra-class state but of working class democracy. The representatives of the Workers' Councils are the foundation of economic and political authority. Therefore the working class will have the decisive voice in conflicts between the political parties. There will also exist an organization which represents actual power —the workers' militia—but unlike its present role, this military force will not be anti-working class but directly linked to the working class.

We believe that all this will give the workers a decisive voice in the state and will safeguard it against rightist danger. We shall not argue with the thesis that the working class in our country represents a reactionary force since it is a meaningless anti-working class bias.

Indeed, the fact that our program is based on working class leadership has also provoked criticism in academic circles. It was said that we advocate workers' power without any participation of other social classes, that our program is anti-intelligentsia, that it is not "modern."

We are convinced that these critics do not really believe in the model of the "general national state" which does not, and most likely will never, exist anywhere outside the program of the PUWP.

Perhaps their criticism means that we failed to mention the forms of political representation within the framework of the workers' state, of society as a whole. These forms, however, are difficult to anticipate. We did not intend to write a future constitution, but a political program. In the nature of things we could only include what is decisive for the character of workers' democracy.

Since the industrial sector plays the decisive role in the economy, the power over industrial production and over labor is tantamount, in modern society, to class rule and political power. As long as there exist in society large groups of people with different positions in the process of production and different social and material positions, parliament or any other national system of representation will sanction the rule of that class which actually controls the activity of labor and the division of the product in the decisive sectors of the economy. That is why abolishing the exploitation of the working class presupposes the assumption of state power by the working class. It is, therefore, sheer nonsense to charge workers' democracy with its class character. It can only be accused of being *working class*. It is a charge levelled from the position of another class, one contending for power.

We are not acquainted with any "modern society" which our adversaries oppose to workers' democracy. Since such a society is neither a bureaucratic dictatorship nor neo-capitalist, they probably mean a technocracy. We do not see why, in that kind of system, the role of the intelligentsia would be larger than in a workers' democracy. As long as exploitation exists there must also be the means to protect it (political police, propaganda, etc.) as well as an apologetic function for scholarship and culture. Each system based on an enslaved working class also deprives intellectuals, one way or another, of their freedom. Only the liberation of the working class will change this state of affairs. In its very nature, workers' democracy must provide much greater freedom for the intelligentsia than exists in the most parliamentary bourgeois democracy, in the most "modern" managerial kingdom.

THE SHARPEST ATTACKS WERE DIRECTED at our practical proposals ("What Is To Be Done?") concerning strike action and the organization of workers' circles, nuclei of the future party. Distorting our analysis and hardly mentioning our program, the official reporters quoted profusely from our last section in order to provoke an indignant reaction to our attempts to violate the criminal laws. Since this relieves us of the need to report the details of that chapter, we shall limit ourselves to restating our position and refuting the objections.

We believe that the economic and social crisis must lead inevitably to revolution. Bureaucratic rule today does not rest on social support but only on its capacity to disorganize the social forces violently by atomizing a working class that is deprived of a party and a program.

Revolution is necessary for social progress, but its course and results would depend on the degree of preparation of the working class. Preparation could serve to limit the confusion associated with revolution and permit its peaceful course with minimum costs for society. If deprived of its own party and its program the working class could not play the leading role in the revolution; if it had neither party nor program, the working class would only bring to power a new oppressor.

For the sake of the whole society, then, the working class must become "a class for itself," conscious of its goals and politically organized. This can be achieved only by *conscious activity* which we consider the political and moral duty of all who want to fight in the interest of the working class. This activity should aim primarily at heightening the political consciousness of the working class, and systematizing its interests into a program. This calls for programmatic discussions and involving factory workers in the struggle for their immediate interests by strike action culminating in the organization of workers' parties and unions.

It has been pointed out, indignantly, that all this is illegal; against the laws of the country. Let us be candid about it. Neither strikes nor the discussion of political programs is prohibited by law. It is true, however, that the present criminal code, created or maintained by the bureaucracy, allows for police persecution for such activities. We have in our country the Criminal Code of 1932, a tool of the semi-fascist "Sanacja" dictatorship and the Small Criminal Code, the tool of the Stalinist dictatorship. Both these Codes, the Small one particularly, are so vague and elastic that, in practice, repressive measures can be applied at will. Therefore, we can see strike organizers punished by law, although strikes are not forbidden, or the participant in a discussion arrested, although discussions are permitted, or the writer of a private letter held, although everybody writes letters.

In talking about legality, it should be mentioned that the basic legal document is the Constitution. But the criminal law (especially the MKK) is in flagrant contradiction to the Constitution. Preventive censorship is unconstitutional, as are all steps taken against freedom of speech, assembly, publication. The very power of the bureaucracy is unconstitutional as well. From the constitutional point of view, strikes, political discussions and organizing workers are not against the law, but against the prevailing lawlessness.

Our motive was not to defend the Constitution, but to commit ourselves to the struggle for the liberation of the working class and of society. Since we are charged, however, with actions which are contrary to the law, we had to demonstrate that the law is interpreted by the powers-that-be and by their defenders in an arbitrary way: what is convenient is mandatory. In reality, therefore, we are charged not with acting against the law, but against the arbitrary prohibitions used by the bureaucratic state power. This kind of morality, which allows one to do only that which the government allows, raises obedience to the rank of the highest virtue and is alien to us in view of our commitment and our traditions. Despite bourgeois prohibitions the KPP [Communist Party of Poland] worked illegally underground; despite prohibitions by the bureaucratic state power, the Communist Left Opposition was active in the USSR and fought the evolving totalitarian Stalinist dictatorship. All groups and parties which fought anti-popular dictatorships for the emancipation of the working class acted in this way. People who are not interested in the class struggle and who consider Marxist analysis to be anachronistic in the modern world, but who, at the same time, attacked us for offenses against Party censorship, and today, for offenses against the discipline imposed by the power of the state, have gone through quite a reversal in their thinking. Brought up under dogmatic Marxism, they have rejected Marxism but retained the dogma; they doubt the value of the Marxist theory of classes, but they have no doubt that there can be no factions in the Party and that the powers-that-be must be obeyed.

We are of the opinion that the present letter will contribute toward overcoming any misinformation about our paper and that it will enable Party members and members of the SYU at the university to have an honest discussion of our theses. We would also like to believe that this time the University Committee of the SYU, being in possession of their own copies of the open letter, will allow those it is really addressed to —i.e., all interested members of both organizations—to acquaint themselves with its text.

We do not know, of course, whether the authorities will decide, as a result of this letter, to apply repressive administrative measures to us or to try us in court. We consider, however, that we have *every right* to address ourselves to the political organizations which removed us from their ranks with the present open letter, which explains to the membership at large of both organizations our views and the motives for our actions.

★ Published at the same time:

SOLIDARNOSC FROM GDANSK TO MILITARY REPRESSION
Colin Barker and Kara Weber

On 13 December 1981 Jaruzelski's army moved in to crush Solidarnosc. The most powerful worker's movement in Europe since the war was halted in its tracks.
How could it happen?
Drawing on a variety of original Polish material Colin Barker and Kara Weber trace the unfolding crisis and the debates it provoked within Solidarnosc.
They argue that Solidarnosc was too deeply rooted in the factories to be co-opted, that real revolutionary possibilities existed, but tragically, this was only realised by the radical wing of Solidarnosc too late.
£1.95 plus 30p postage

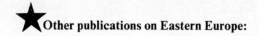Other publications on Eastern Europe:

BUREAUCRACY AND REVOLUTION IN EASTERN EUROPE
by Chris Harman
East Germany 1953, Poland 1956, Hungary 1956, Czechoslovakia 1968,
Poland 1970 .. this book looks at how Eastern Europe turned 'Communist' and
at the turbulent relationship between workers and regimes ever since.
Written before the present upheaval in Poland, but indispensible for
understanding the background to those events.
£2.50 plus 50p postage.

STATE CAPITALISM IN RUSSIA
by Tony Cliff
Russia today is a centre of reaction as vicious and almost as powerful as the
US—and as capitalist. What is state capitalism? How did it come about? Why
is Russia not a workers' state? Tony Cliff's book has become the classic
analysis.
£1.00 plus 50p postage

RUSSIA: HOW THE REVOLUTION WAS LOST
by Alan Gibbons
In 1917, for the first time in world history, a workers' government took power in
Russia. Out of the bloodbath of the First World War an alternative and better
society was born. Within 20 years it was dead, murdered by a new class, a new
despot—Stalin. Why did it happen? This pamphlet gives some of the answers ...
50p plus 20p postage/ten for £4 post free

THE GREAT LIE
by Abbie Bakan
Today a great lie dominates the world—that socialism already exists. This
'socialism' offers no alternative to capitalism. Instead we see Soviet 'socialist'
tanks occupying Afghanistan and threatening the workers of Poland; thousands
of boat people forced to flee 'socialist' Vietnam. This pamphlet shows what
socialism *is,* and what it is *not.*
Originally published by the International Socialists, Canada.
75p plus 20p postage/ten for £6.50 post free.

Available from good left bokshops, or by post from:
BOOKMARKS, 265 Seven Sisters Road, Finsbury Park, London N4 2DE.

★ BOOKMARKS

is a socialist bookshop in North London, where you'll find two floors of books on socialism, trade unionism, workers' history, women's issues, economics, internationalism, socialist fiction ... and much more.

You'll find us at 265 Seven Sisters Road, just round the corner from Finsbury Park tube station. If you live too far away to call in, we also run a socialist mail order service—so write for our free booklists.

Month by month during the development of Solidarity *Socialist Review* has provided coverage unequalled in English. That has been only part of the regular in depth coverage *Socialist Review* gives on the class struggle both in Britain and internationally. Essential reading for every activist.

Individual subscriptions for 12 issues: Britain and Ireland £7.50, Overseas Surface £8.50, Europe Air £10, Elsewhere Air £12 (institutions add £4).

☆ The fighting weekly socialist newspaper

Special introductory offer: 10 issues for just £2 (including postage)
Normal subscription rates: six months £7★ one year £13
From: SW Circulation, PO Box 82, London E2. (Cheques/POs made out to
Larkham Printers and Publishers)